IMAGES OF ENGLAND

AROUND SHREWSBURY
VOLUME II

IMAGES OF ENGLAND

AROUND SHREWSBURY
VOLUME II

DEREK M. WALLEY

TEMPUS

To Joshua, Katharine and Jessica

Frontispiece: Robert Darlow of Woodbank Villa, Exfords Green. This photograph, taken in around 1938, shows the rabbit catcher kitted out ready for his next assignment. This well-known local character carries an array of now illegal gin traps, together with a selection of other tools of his trade heaped on his wheelbarrow; including sacks, snares and spade, watched over by his trusty rough-haired terrier.

First published 2004

Tempus Publishing Limited
The Mill, Brimscombe Port,
Stroud, Gloucestershire, GL5 2QG
www.tempus-publishing.com

British Library Cataloguing in Publication Data.
A catalogue record for this book is available from the British Library.

ISBN 0 7524 3371 7

Typesetting and origination by Tempus Publishing Limited.
Printed in Great Britain.

Contents

	Acknowledgements	6
	Introduction	7
one	Shrewsbury	11
two	The Condover Hundred	43
three	Longnor and Leebotwood	51
four	Historic Pitchford and Acton Burnell	65
five	The Severn Valley	75
six	Allscott and Admaston	89
seven	North West to Shawbury	97
eight	Baschurch and the River Perry	107
nine	The Rea and the Stiperstones	117

Acknowledgements

The compilation of this book has led to my delving into an archive of printed material gathered over many years. An opportunity has also been taken to thoroughly scrutinise and select from an accumulation of mainly Edwardian-era postcards and Victorian cartes de visite. I would particularly like to thank a nucleus of friends with similar interests, who have willingly furnished me with some little gems, without which this publication would have been significantly poorer. I mention in no specific order David Woodhouse; David and Elizabeth Benson; Chris Davies; John Ruscoe and Simon Maiden of Abbeycolour. My special thanks go to Eileen Owen; Jim and Leslie Rhodes; Peter and Nora Lewis; and all those local informants who, without hesitation, answered my questions and gave me much additional information during visits to each of the villages highlighted.

Finally, I readily recognise the fact that a high percentage of the images used within these pages were formerly part of a large and unprecedented accumulation of postcards collected over more than twenty-five years by the late Sheila Hart, a knowledgeable and much respected adopted Salopian.

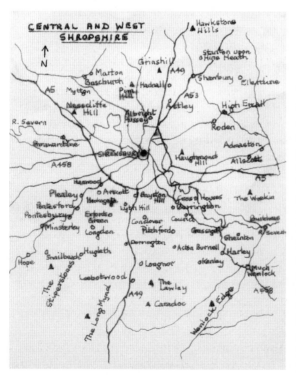

This map details those villages situated around the county town of Shrewsbury which are portrayed within these pages. Geographically, most are placed to the south in a wide arc from the Hope Valley in the west to Cressage and Harley in the east. Many of these villages border Shropshire hill country, an area historically interesting, particularly from an architectural viewpoint. Numerous agricultural and domestic buildings being worthy of note. The villages to the east and north form part of the extended Cheshire Plain, the land hereabouts being kinder and more forgiving.

Introduction

Shropshire – A Brief History

After the sacking of Roman Uriconium (Wroxeter) by the Saxons, the Britons retired to seek a place of refuge on the higher reaches of the River Severn. They were to find shelter on high ground within a large meander of the river, at what was soon to become known as Pengwerne – literally meaning a head or hill of alders. This chosen place, no doubt at that time surrounded by marshland, was considered to be suitable to defend against possible intruders. This change of site is likely to have taken place in around AD 570, 150 years after the Romans abandoned Britain. However, the Saxons were to continue their plundering and it was not long before the Britons were forced to leave their new-found stronghold for the sanctuary of the high mountains of Wales. Thus the destruction of Uriconium was to have a direct correlation with the establishment of early Shrewsbury.

As a result the Saxons were in command of most of the Kingdom of Powis, with Pengwerne at its centre. The legendary Offa was next on the scene and, as King of Mercia, consolidated the position, particularly with his lengthy earth entrenchment to deter the marauding Welsh. This took place in around AD 757-796 and large parts of the earthwork remain in place today. The Saxons were to rename Pengwerne 'Scrobbes-byrig', meaning an area of high ground overgrown with scrub. Anglo-Saxon and Anglo-Danish kings established a mint here and after the Norman Conquest coins were continuously struck up to Henry IIIs reign (1216-1272) and again during the reign of Charles I (1625-1649).

At the time of the Norman subversion, the Welsh laid siege to the town's castle stronghold, burning and pillaging in their wake. Retribution was swift. Roger de Montgomery was appointed absolute overlord of Mercia and Earl of Shrewsbury. His first act was to build a new castle stronghold, from which Roger set forth to administer his newly-acquired province and, above all, suppress the belligerent Welsh. Roger de Montgomery died in 1094 but power struggles continued, Henry I appointing a succession of viceroys to govern his far-flung province.

The Plantagenets, from Henry II (1154–1189) onwards, introduced and maintained a system of taxation and the new procedure of trial by jury, which replaced the barbaric practices of trial by battle or by justification. Taxes collected by the sheriff were not popular with the burgesses or the townsfolk. These arbitrarily levied monies were often subject to the extortions of the sheriff and his officers. During the reign of Richard I a fixed annual rent became an alternative and more popular method of payment. In 1199 King John granted Shrewsbury two new charters which basically set down new privileges or sanctions. A Common Council was authorised, together with the appointment of a town provost or magistrate; a further attempt to uphold the law. Perhaps more interestingly, a third charter was granted in 1205 which allowed the town's burgesses to hold a fair for three days in June of each year.

King John gave his daughter, Johanna, in marriage to Prince Llewellyn the Great, together with the title Lordship of Ellesmere. But clashes continued. Shrewsbury was attacked and taken by Llewellyn in 1215, only to return to the King's control the following year, after yet more bloodshed.

Shrewsbury, in its strategic position high above the Severn, remained at the centre of the feuding between the English and the Welsh. Henry III granted a patent to the town in 1220 allowing the burgesses to collect tolls and so help pay for the defence of the 'frontier'. Approval from the monarch was also given by the monarch to the building of defensive walls, and Henry paid periodic visits to Shrewsbury to see for himself how things were progressing. Skirmishing, accompanied by arson and looting, continued to be a common occurrence in the Shropshire countryside, the Welsh only withdrawing when they suddenly found a superior royalist force massed against them.

It has to be concluded that these experiences should have a profound effect upon the townsfolk and, therefore, it is little wonder that they were to become staunch Royalists, a deep-seated loyalty which at times proved costly in terms of damage to property and loss of lives. Through the burgesses, Henry III allowed the setting up of merchant guilds, membership of which allowed open trading within the town's precincts. Surely a precursor of the annual musical and floral fête!

Things were to change greatly following the succession of Edward I in 1272. Unable to placate Llewellyn, Edward decided on the annexation of Wales and commenced military operations four years later, the conflict eventually resulting in the Prince's death in 1282. The outcome was rather overwhelming as far as Shrewsbury was concerned; not only did Edward encamp his armies around the town but he also transferred the seat of government here in 1277, bringing with him his complete entourage of King's Bench justices and Barons of the Exchequer. The village of Acton Burnell was to play a major role in this relocation of power. The very first 'national convention' took place at Shrewsbury in 1283, when the Commons participated in a share of legal authority, together with earls, barons and knights from each county, plus representatives from every city and major town in the kingdom. Shrewsbury, therefore, witnessed the earliest legitimate popular representation within the constitution. Thereafter, the town was to lose the importance it had acquired as the centre of territorial hostility and soon reverted to what might be termed a more ordinary municipality!

The next local happening of any import was the Battle of Shrewsbury in July 1403, when Henry IV was to achieve victory over the insurgents under Henry Percy 'Hotspur', son of the Duke of Northumberland. His descendents include the Heber-Percy's of Hodnet Hall. The aftermath of the battle included the beheading at Shrewsbury of the Earl of Worcester, Sir Richard Venables and Sir Richard Vernon. Perhaps more prosaically, Henry agreed to the founding of a college or chantry on the site of the battlefield, the cost being met by tithes collected from numerous parishes. Of this institution, the church of St Mary Magdalene survives to this day.

The coming of the Tudors in 1485 was to bring peace but a less glamorous reign. King Henry VII was very much a businessman who signed trade agreements and supported seafaring voyages of discovery. In so doing, he brought wealth to his country, though it was to be somewhat squandered by his son, Henry VIII. In 1536 began the Dissolution of the Monasteries. At the same time Henry was to throw off the yoke of the Church of Rome. This latter act being rooted solely in Henry's inability to obtain permission from that quarter for his requested divorce from Catherine of Aragon. This act was to be spectacularly important for the future of his country, for it led to the establishment of the protestant Church of England.

In Shropshire, Henry's greatest legacy must be the presence of the many ruined abbeys. Some of the monies derived from this spoliation were later to be used in the founding of the Shrewsbury Free Grammar School in Castle Gates in1551.

The reign of Elizabeth I (1558-1603) was one of considerable commercial growth, as well as a period of intellectual advancement in literature and undoubted naval supremacy on the High Seas. This latter competency culminated in the defeat of the Spanish Armada by Admiral's Drake, Frobisher, Raleigh and others. The penchant of the Tudors to design and build outstanding town houses and country mansions remains evident for all to see in any perambulation around scenic Shropshire. Pitchford Hall (1570) is especially imposing, as is Plaish Hall (1580), the likely first brick building in the county. Upper Corvedale's dignified Shipton Hall, built of Wenlock limestone and dated 1587, is another fine example; whilst Shrewsbury town centre retains many period merchant's houses.

The next unfortunate chapter in English history was to begin in August 1642 with open hostilities between King and Parliament. The Civil War had begun! Inevitably individuals, organisations and complete geographical areas were quick to take sides. Shropshire was mostly to take the King's side, the North East of the county being the notable exception. Justices, clergy and numerous large landowners were quick to sign a declaration of loyalty and Sir Francis Ottley of Pitchford was appointed Shrewsbury's Governor; other staunch royalists included Sir Vincent Corbett, the Newport's of High Ercall, Thomas Scriven of Frodesley and the Whitmore's, the Acton's and the More's of south Shropshire. Their opponents supporting the parliamentary cause included Thomas Hunt of Boreatton, Robert Clive of Styche, Market Drayton, and Thomas Mytton of Halston, Whittington.

Charles I came to Wellington and Shrewsbury in 1642, no doubt to drum up support. The war itself was to see much posturing, sieges and acts of wanton destruction. Much of the large scale military unpleasantries were to take place outside Shropshire, notably at Edgehill and Marston Moor. Well documented, less conspicuous local operations were those at Hopton Castle, High Ercall, Ellesmere, Oswestry, Albright Hussey, Stokesay and, ultimately Bridgnorth and Ludlow. These last two market towns were the location of royalist capitulations which more or less signalled the end of hostilities in Shropshire. The Battle of Worcester in 1650 was to be another royalist defeat and the story of the King's subsequent escape and secretion at Boscobel on the Shropshire/Staffordshire border is well known. The Civil War had effectively ended, a constitutional monarchy being the end result.

The Act of Uniformity was passed in 1662, declaring that every minister of the church shall proclaim his unfeigned assent and consent to everything contained in the Book of Common Prayer. Pious men of liberty and conscience had been fighting in a peaceful manner for their own particular cause over many years and the new Act had the immediate effect of strengthening and formalising their non-conformism. These dissenting voices objected to the power of the bishops and high church ceremonial; the complete reform of the Church from grass roots upwards being their overall objective. Persecution was the direct result, with fifty-eight Shropshire clergymen losing their ministries, many being formally ejected from their livings.

The poor state of the roads in the seventeenth- and eighteenth-centuries had done nothing to help the operation of long-distance coach operations. Journeys were long and arduous and by 1800 the average speed of these horse-drawn vehicles was twelve miles per hour. Shrewsbury was to become a main coaching centre and the problems became even more emphasised with the advent of the Penny Post in 1840. In 1787 Thomas Telford was appointed Surveyor of Public Works for Shropshire, responsible for improving the main trunk routes as well as the numerous new bridges, both within the county and elsewhere. Many of Telford's bridges have withstood the ravages of time, whether they are of stone like Montford Bridge (1792), or cast-iron like Cound Arbour (1797) and Cantlop (1813). One specific brief handed to Telford was to upgrade the London to Holyhead road, which passes directly through the county. He also diversified into canal engineering and was the designer of the first cast-iron aqueduct at Longdon upon Tern, as well as engineer in charge of the Ellesmere to Llangollen Canal of 1793 and responsible for the fine aqueduct at Pontcysyllte, just across the county border. Yet another of Telford's accomplishments was church design, with St Mary Magdalene, Bridgnorth, of 1792.

Shrewsbury and Shropshire were to see many more changes in the nineteenth and twentieth centuries. Extraordinary progress was to be made in several different spheres. The railways arrived in Shropshire in 1848, serving most of the larger market towns some twenty years later. The horse and cart era was swiftly coming to an end and the population was rapidly taking advantage of the more efficient form of transportation. They could now explore well beyond their immediate neighbourhood and trade and commerce were also quick to benefit from a new found ease in searching out new outlets for the goods they had for sale. Far more importantly, this advancement helped nourish the already glowing embers of the Industrial Revolution, a British transformation which had its origins firmly based here in Shropshire, particularly in the Severn Gorge and Coalbrookdale.

In the eighteenth century Shrewsbury had become an elegant and fashionable town, with its streets bordered by tastefully-styled merchant's houses, public and Church buildings. The Victorians and Edwardians were later to make their mark. Their pursuit of pleasure soon led to organised social events, for example flower and agricultural shows and the building of theatres for light entertainment. Manufacturing industry came to the county town in 1915, thus improving local job prospects. The engineering firm of Alley and MacLellan arrived from Polmadie, Glasgow, where they had been building steam wagons since 1905. They quickly expanded on a large site in the northern suburbs. The firm built a housing complex for its workers in the early 1920s and the 'Sentinel' became a renowned machine exported all over the world. Petrol and diesel engine vehicles were to follow alongside their steam driven companions from the mid-1930s.

Although much of Shrewsbury's past has been irretrievably lost by neglect or vandalism, a significant portion of our local heritage has been saved and will hopefully be diligently guarded by future generations. The county town stands at the centre of an area of fertile farmland but its agricultural importance may possibly have diminished over the years. It remains an important administrative centre and a magnet for shoppers from the Welsh Marches area. Its transport links are not what they were a half century ago and it is no longer considered meaningful to support its previous status as a major junction on the railway network. Direct services to London are also considered to be a thing of the past.

The good news is that some competent amateur and professional photographers had the foresight to record on film many of Shropshire's historic buildings, period street scenes and former personalities. It is solely because of their vision that a few little gems from the past are able to be reproduced within the succeeding pages.

one

Shrewsbury

E nveloped by the river, dominated by its castle, the county town still retains many of its Tudor period merchant's houses. The increasing wealth of the nineteenth century, based on agriculture, led to prosperous professionals erecting residences of Georgian and Regency splendour, thus greatly adding to the urban landscape. Many of these fine houses survive and, together with numerous attractive terraced villas, contribute to the all-round ambience of the capital of the Marches.

Previous page top: Victorian calling cards. A montage of the reverse side of some Shrewsbury cartes de visite. The obverse side of these early examples of the work of local photographers was invariably based on studio studies of family groups or individuals. Street scenes and buildings are less common but do date back to the 1860s.

Previous page below: Shrewsbury Free Grammar School, School Gardens, 1875. These buildings date back to 1594 and comprise a chapel, library and gallery as well as classrooms. They are of Grinshill freestone and have been much altered over the years, especially between 1815 and 1831. The public school moved to Kingsland in 1882 and the accommodation was taken over by the Borough Library and Museums Service. Complete restoration was undertaken by the County Council in the early 1980s and now forms part of the Libraries and Information Services. The former playground area looks rather bare without its shrubberies and statue of Charles Darwin.

Above: The Cross Keys, High Street, 1869. Situated at the bottom of Grope Lane, a group of children gather outside, presumably at the behest of the photographer. In 1780 the ale house on this site was known as The Globe but by 1820 was renamed the Cross Keys. It ceased to be a licensed house by 1913. The building, currently used as a coffee house, is timber-framed, dates from the late sixteenth century, and has fortunately retained its multi-decorative quatrefoils.

Right: Owen's Mansion, High Street, 1869. The west end of this attractive building was at this time in dual use. Firstly, by John Evans as an early hairdressing salon, whilst Robert Slaney, a wine and spirit dealer established next door, appears to be about to receive the delivery of a firkin of sherry. The timber-framing here dates from 1570.

Above, left: No. 40 Pride Hill. The shops of William H. Reece, tobacconist, and James Deaves, clothier, are shown on this 1885 photograph. This early sixteenth century timber-framed building has somehow survived the modernisation processes of the 1950s and '60s. It remains largely unaltered to this day but now specialises in serving chocolate treats. The decorated barge-boards and the cusped quatrefoil panels are special features but the small balustrade balconies are rather recent additions, dating from around 1900.

Left: St Mary's Church, its tower partly hidden by the old water storage reservoir, 1869. This substantial elevated storage tank placed at the highest point in the town centre was necessary to maintain a suitable mains water supply. A landmark for miles around, it was positioned behind the Drapers Almshouses which, until the 1960s, formed part of the street scene in St Mary's Street. The photographer was Josiah Groom of Wyle Cop who actually pointed his camera through the uncompleted dial of the then newly erected clock tower of the Market Hall.

Right: High Street. This late 1920s street scene shows business premises opposite the Square with motorcars beginning to dominate things. All would now be illegally parked and also driven the wrong way up a one-way thoroughfare! Alberta Batsford advertises her wares high up on a building gable.

Below: No. 6 Market Street. Alberta Batsford removed from High Street to Market Street in the late 1920s. This publicity handout shows the double frontage display of these premises in 1935. At different times the latest ladies fashions were on sale at shops bearing her name at Walker Street, Wellington, and no. 54 Sandford Avenue, Church Stretton.

ALBERTA BATSFORD LTD.

THE FASHION SPECIALISTS FOR COATS · DRESSES · MILLINERY · KNITWEAR

6 MARKET STREET, SHREWSBURY - - and at WALKER STREET, WELLINGTON

Telephone 3274   Telephone 139

Alberta Batsford, ladies' outfitters, 1915. Alberta Batsford, on the right in long skirt and blouse, stands outside her Church Stretton premises at no. 54 Sandford Avenue, together with a lady sales assistant. The identity of the children is not known. The quality and modernity of the offerings in her retail premises was beyond reproach. Miss Alberta Louise Batsford resided for many years at Church Stretton, firstly at Redcote, Central Avenue, and later at Knollcrest, Trevor Hill.

Right: Hills Lane, 1912. Situated between Mardol and Barker Street this narrow thoroughfare of cobbles and granite setts must have been a busy place at the time this photograph was taken. The Olde Gullet Inn, on the left at nos 2 and 3, was de-licensed in 1942. Rowley's Mansion can be seen in the middle background; beyond and elsewhere in the near vicinity was a preponderance of small town dwellings, all of low standard and variously described as hovels and shacks being only fit for razing to the ground – an act completed in the 1950s.

Below: Female Post Office staff, 29 September 1916. During the hostilities of the First World War the General Post Office employed many female workers to help in the collection and distribution of post. This postcard shows some of Shrewsbury's uniformed contingent. The sender of the postcard, George, complains to his lady friend in Scarborough 'that things are not as they should be, the week ending balances are always wrong.'

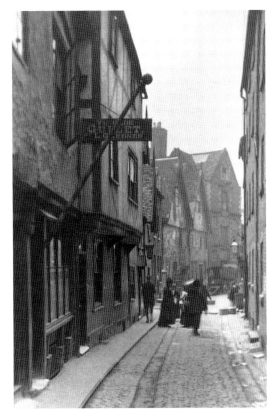

The Ship Inn yard, 1905.

Rowley's Mansion. Artist Emily Hay was born Emily Henshaw at Oswestry in 1824 and married Walter Cecil Hay, professor of music and choirmaster at Shrewsbury St Chad, in 1855. The family lived at various addresses in the town including Dogpole Court. Emily's oil paintings must have been of a special quality for she exhibited five paintings at the Royal Birmingham Society of Artists between 1875 and 1879. Her favoured subjects were cathedrals, castles and coastal scenes. However, these two local snow scenes, of buildings within a stone's throw of each other, off Hills Lane, have a slightly different theme. Perhaps Emily, or a small local printer, considered them to be of sufficient merit to publish them as postcards in 1905. Other examples of Emily's town snowscapes continue to come to light.

William Bratton, 1904. Mr Bratton was well known locally as a virtuoso on the violin. He was tutor to many local budding musicians and is said to have taught the young Sir Edward German, son of the organist/choirmaster at Whitchurch Congregational Church. German later wrote the patriotic operetta *Merrie England*. In the late nineteenth century William Bratton was also employed as what would now be termed a peripatetic assistant music teacher at Shrewsbury School.

Bratton's Music Shop, Dogpole. The business started life in Great Yarmouth in around 1910 and the location shown in this 1960s photograph was the second such site in Dogpole, the piano workshops being in Mardol. The business passed to William's son, Richard, and ultimately to his grandson, another Richard who died in 2002. The business has recently closed and the premises are undergoing alteration. In August 1976 the shop was gutted by fire which also caused damage to the adjoining premises of John Rea, Photographic Studios.

Right: Fish Street and St Julian's Church, 1912. This photograph, without its now permanent accompaniment of parked cars, shows the Three Fishes Inn on the right, Shrewsbury's first non-smoking pub. Once surrounded by butchers' shops and now fondly known as 'The Fishes', it was formerly a small town house of the late fifteenth century; timber framed with a jettied upper storey, it was first recorded as an inn in 1780 and appears to have prospered ever since.

Below: The Three Fishes Inn at no. 4 Fish Street. The then licensee, William Sparling, requests payment of a bill for the hire of cutlery and tumblers from Simon Richards in October 1888. Total cost 9s 10d.

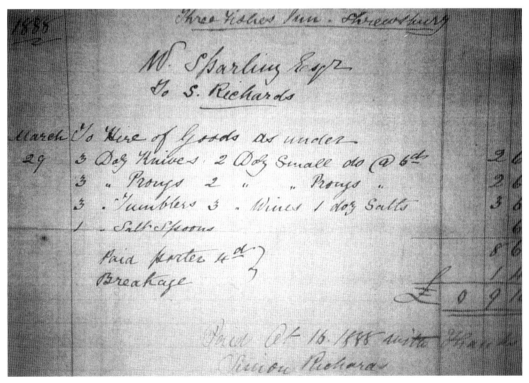

Pride Hill, *c.* 1900. This street is now more or less pedestrianised, as it was in this snapshot taken over a century ago. Horse-drawn delivery carts prevail, as seen on the right outside Bagnall and Blowers grocery and provisions shop at no. 20.

Product promotion, Bagnall and Blower, 1907. This postcard illustrates a delightful way of getting to your potential customers. It would be fair to assume that the wife of the Revd Frederick Townend of Shrawardine Rectory was well-equipped to fully exploit the annual arrival of Seville oranges in this country. The good reverend was in his twilight years spending them as vicar of rural Montford with Shrawardine from 1906-09.

Above, right: The High Cross, 1906. This rather fuzzy photograph looking down Castle Street, previously known as High Pavement, shows no hint of Marks and Spencers 1d bazaar. The premises on the left include John Goodwin (Hairdresser), Warner and Hitchin (Stationer), John Marsh (Watchmaker) and Arthur Dyer/ Bon Marché (Draper). The latter premises were, in 1909, to form the basis of a new branch for this well-known national retailer.

Below: Bon Marché, nos 5 and 6 Castle Street, 1907. This central and extensive property of Arthur Dyer, draper, silk mercer and milliner, is shown on this promotional photograph. Two years later, this three-storey building became completely unrecognisable following conversion into a branch of Marks and Spencer. In more recent times, expansion has meant the incorporation of the former Littlewoods property next door.

Wilding & Son Ltd, Castle Street, Stag Dinner, Christmas, *c.* 1955. It is thought that this event was held at the old Office Inn in Milk Street, and the immediate thought has to be why are there no lady members of staff present? Those sitting include: Jack Wilding, fourth from left, proprietor; Sam Boon, fourth from right, works manager; and Dennis Bridges, first right, foreman in the binding department. Amongst those standing are Bill Elson from Chavel, Ford, Phil Taylor who lived in Longden Road, David Trumper, ex-school teacher and local historian, plus Reg Evans from Belle Vue Gardens.

The Raven Hotel, Castle Street, 1910. It is likely that an inn existed on this site from 1521. The raven emblem relates to past ownership by the Corbet family, whose family crest it still is. This postcard illustrates the street's loss of this highly attractive hostelry with its gothic style windows and decorative Victorian verandas. In the age of steam, hotel guests were picked up and returned to the railway station by hansom cab. It was a favourite abode of American servicemen, being used as a rest and leave club from the spring of 1943 until early 1945.

COCKTAIL BAR — PRICE LIST

COCKTAILS

Dry Martini	...	3/-
Bronx	...	3/-
Manhattan...	...	3/-
White Lady	...	3/-
Side Car	...	4/-
Pussyfoot ...	...	2/-
John Collins	...	3/-
Gin Fizz	...	3/-
Gin Sour	...	3/-
Whisky Sour	...	3/6
Pimm's No. 1	...	4/-

PORT and SHERRIES

Sherry	...	3/-
Old Monk Port	...	2/6
Adams " 15 "	...	3/-

SPIRITS

Gin	... ...	2/-
Whisky	...	2/3
Rum	... ...	2/-
Brandy XXX	...	3/-

LIQUEURS

From	... ...	3/-

BOTTLED BEERS

Light Ales ...	...	1/5
Other Beers	...	1/6
Nips Beer ...	...	1/-
Pilsener Lager	...	1/10

Tomato Juice	...	1/3
Pineapple Juice	...	1/3
Moussec	...	2/6

As Shrewsbury's leading Hotel, the Raven offers first class cuisine and wines. It is the rendezvous of the County, and an ideal centre for visiting the beautiful and historic countryside.

THE RAVEN HOTEL
SHREWSBURY

Telephone 4414-5

The New **COCKTAIL BAR** really repays a visit, for it has been built in **VAULTS**, which in the fifteenth century, were parts of the site of a Monastery.

Above and below: The Raven Hotel, publicity and advertising card, 1950s. Printed by Walkers of Fish Street, this small notelet is rather informative of prices in the Raven's delightful cocktail bar. The dance floor, whilst on the small side, was also a pleasant place to while away a few hours polishing up dance steps and improving chat-up lines. Grid-puzzle enthusiasts are invited to have a bit of fun solving the Raven's teaser.

ACROSS

1 and 6. We really advise a visit here.
7. Appears twice during an innings.
8. A most popular bird, but not for the table.
10. Note well, in short, the initials of a French Emperor.
13. A small drink as clean as a new pin in reverse.
14. Difficult to do once in the Cocktail Bar.
15. Up after this for a first course in the Restaurant.
16. Oh, la, as a Frenchman would say.
17. A German cheer for a Rhine special.
18. Naturally follows after an appetiser in 1 and 6.
19. You will yearn for a " tall " drink when thirsty.
22. Brandy 12-17 years old.
23. " No horses," see also 18 down.

DOWN

1. The R.A.C. is naturally interested in its reversal.
2. Gin and this make a fine appetiser.
3. Your appetite after a visit to 1 and 6.
4. Descriptive of our food and drinks.
5. Dr. Johnson said nothing has produced such happiness as an . . . .
9. A popular sort of cap is just the thing (anag.).
11. Cook loses his head and has pages when given another letter.
12. A Shrewsbury meeting place when preceded by 8 across.
15. A kitchen utensil favoured by a journalist.
18 and 23. The hen is partly responsible for these drinks.
20 and 21. It is mid-day when 21 comes before 20.

And finally, 16, 1, 6, 8 and 12 discloses Shropshire's favourite rendezvous

Visit of King George V, the Market Square, 1914. The King was a visitor to Shrewsbury and the Royal Agricultural Society's Show at the racecourse, Monkmoor, on Friday 3 July 1914. The show, which now has a permanent showground at Stoneleigh in Warwickshire, had been to Shrewsbury twice before, in 1845 and 1884. The Royal Train arrived at the station at 12.45 p.m., after which the King proceeded by open landau up Castle Gates and down Pride Hill to the Market Square followed by military and civic dignitaries. Parked alongside the statue of Clive of India, various addresses were given by the King and civic worthies. His Majesty, by simulation, then laid the foundation stone for the new library building at Shrewsbury School. The King and his entourage then left for the showground, on the way passing alongside the Abbey Church where massed choirs sang the National Anthem. At the showground war veterans were presented to His Majesty and, following luncheon, the royal guest toured the various exhibits and watched the show-jumping. The Royal Train left Shrewsbury on its return journey at 4.45 p.m. How things have moved on, the open fields of the show site is now a mass of suburban housing.

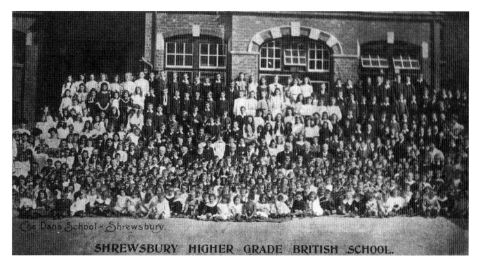

The Dana School, 1906. The complete school roll appears to have been brought together in this Wilding book postcard. The school was opened in 1813 on a site under Castle Hill at the rear of the county gaol. A change of name to the Lancasterian School in 1907 appears to be a rather belated recognition of the good deeds of the Quaker pioneer educationist, Joseph Lancaster. Undoubtedly the best-known headmaster of the school was Mr T.G. Robin who held the position for forty years from 1891. He was to marry his art teacher, Miss Kate Crabb; other teachers remembered are the Misses Smith and Harrison, Mr Wilson who taught maths and Miss Weare who did her best to ensure that everyone knew their French verbs. The school closed in the 1980s.

The Railway Station and Castle, 1905. The horse cabs and delivery drays provide suitable animation for what appears to be a less than busy forecourt scene. Built from Grinshill freestone in a Tudor-Gothic style in 1848, the station building provides a complete contrast to its elevated red sandstone neighbour which dates back to the late eleventh century, and was built by Roger de Montgomery.

Wm. PYE,

Antique Furniture Dealer,

23 to 26, Butcher Row, Shrewsbury.

Old Carved Oak,
Chippendale and Sheraton
Furniture a speciality.

Chair originally belonging to John Mytton, Esq., Holston, Shropshire.

Above and right: William Pye Antiques, Butcher Row, 1911. As its name implies this street was once the centre of the slaughtering and butchery trade and before 1800 a very high percentage of the shops were involved in such gory practices. At the end of the nineteenth century William Pye took over extensive premises on the west side of the street, together with its ornamental columns and top brackets. He was still there twenty years later. Nos 23–26 have since been completely reconstructed and now form part of Owen's Coffee Rooms, although the eighteenth-century buildings on either side continue to make their contribution to the overall urban picture.

Above: Phillips & Co. general supply stores, Butcher Row, 1900. The main entrance was around the corner at no. 35 Pride Hill. The author recalls his father, who worked here as a weekend errand boy during First World War, relating to him how he had tripped and fallen down the hoist opening. He landed on the ground floor covered in flour, sustaining a broken hip. The building, formerly known as Greyhound Chambers, was originally a town house and with its jettied upper storeys dates from the sixteenth century. It has since been much-altered, its Pride Hill frontage being entirely false and of the early twentieth century.

Right: Princess Street, 1932. This 'time exposure' snapshot shows draper David Lloyd's mansion of 1570 and the adjoining business premises of Joseph Lewis Della Porta. All the half-timbered work was very soon to be reduced to rubble when the County Council decided to extend the Shirehall. A street cleaner with his cart ponders awhile and a Ford delivery van stands outside Judge & Sons grocery store.

Charles Chaplin
"THE IDLE CLASS"

CENTRAL HALL, SHREWSBURY.

□.

6 Days Only, Commencing

Monday, Jan. 2nd, 1922

THREE PERFORMANCES
DAILY, 2.40, 6.40 and 8.40

Seats can now be Booked.
Telephone - 295.

Charles Chaplin

IN

"The Idle Class"

THE BEST YET!

Above and left: The Central Hall and Charlie Chaplin. This famous comedian came to Shrewsbury and the Central Hall in 1922 but only on celluloid. Silent films like *The Idle Class* were usually complemented by a piano but a little later roughly synchronised music on a drum disk was the more usual accompaniment. Promotional advertising at this time was virtually confined to the local newspapers; the radio was non-existent and the cinema operators were reduced to handouts, like this example in postcard format.

Above: The Central Hall, Castle Gates. Shrewsbury's first public cinema was situated at no. 17, opposite what is now the Granada Buildings. Adapted from a disused ashlar-faced non-conformist chapel and school erected in 1849, it opened in November 1909 when it was known as the Picturedrome. The façade remains in situ today. Following a failure to comply with the conditions of the Cinematograph Act of that year, the cinema was closed for a brief period and reopened on 24 January 1910 together with a new name, The Central Hall Picture Palace. The owner/lessee until 1928 was Mr Glynn Hill, a gentleman who ran similar enterprises at Wrexham and Chester. From 1928 until closure in 1931, it was run by Mr Josephs and the Black Country Cinema Circuit. It would seem that closure was greatly influenced by a fire which gutted the winding room after the last show on 21 March 1931. This was likely to be only part of the problem; after all, the King's Hall in St Julian's Friars had opened in 1914, followed by a modern Empire Cinema at nos 55-57 Mardol in 1928. Competition had become a little keen!

Right: Mardol Quay, Gethin's Garage and the King's Head Inn, 1938. Edward Gethin, having spent the war years in India, returned to Shrewsbury to set up his garage business on the Quay in 1920/21. His premises, together with the adjacent riverside warehouses, were acquired by the County Council in 1958/59 for road widening purposes. The Hills Arms public house, once forming part of the site, had previously been demolished in 1952. Morris & Co's Morris commercial van, registration UJ 8185, delivers goods to Thomas Smith's shop next to the late fifteenth century timber-framed and jettied Kings Head Inn.

Left: Visit of the Prince of Wales. The future Edward VIII visited the town on 21 June 1932. Accompanied by the Mayor, Alderman M.N. How, he walks in front of the Castle where he had just had lunch with civic dignitaries. The Prince had arrived in a De Haviland Puss Moth, landing at Frank's Farm, Harlescott, at 12.30 p.m. He later visited Shrewsbury School and Copthorne Barracks.

Below: Visit of the Prince of Wales, 21 June 1932. Whilst at Copthorne Barracks, the Prince walked around the British Legion Fair with its stalls and sideshows ranged alongside the central running track. He carried out an inspection of Legion members with their colourful banners and watched a physical training display by soldiers of the King's Shorpshire Light Infantry. Before he took tea with Legion officers he purchased two tickets in a competition for a specially-made commemorative cake. Described as a beautifully made piece of work, it was fashioned to represent an open book with a message moulded in the icing greeting the Prince of Wales. This artistic interpretation is illustrated on this postcard issued to commemorate the occasion.

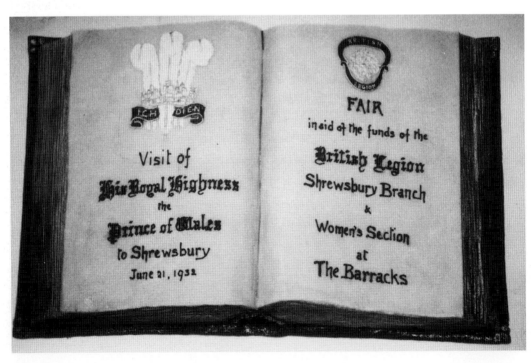

Frankwell, 1905. At this time this architecturally important building was a pair of dwelling houses but soon afterwards the ground floors were converted into shops. Of the early seventeenth century, the timber framing extends to two storeys plus an attic. The outstanding features are the two full-height, projecting square-gabled bays, the mullioned and transomed windows to the first floor and local style balustrade panel mouldings to two floors. Note the single quatrefoil in the gable apex.

Frankwell, 1912. An engaging view with not a motor car in sight. Children play outside Helen Rosier's sweet shop at no. 114, whilst a farmer or dealer winds his way to town in his horse-drawn buggy. The local pig keeper heads the other way with containers full of swill, the results of his morning labours. Besides the String of Horses Inn, top left, identifiable properties on the right-hand side include John Jones, stationer and sub-post master at no. 112, Percy Boswell, grocer at no. 108-109 and the Crown Inn where Henry Gough was licensee at no. 98. The prominent tobacconist signs on the left advertise the premises of Alfred Morris at no. 12. One interesting fact about Frankwell, the Little Borough, was the presence on both sides of the street of numerous passages or shuts leading to small court areas. At this time there were at least twelve in number and some still exist today.

THE ABBEY HOUSE SCHOOL,
SHREWSBURY.

Report of *Norah Lee*

for *Summer* Term *1930.*

SCRIPTURE.	*Fair. H.Mc.G*	
ENGLISH *Composition* *Grammar* *History* *Literature*	*Fair* *Fair.* *Preparation erratic, or work could be better* *Fair. F.Mc.G.*	*B.S* *H.E.W* *D.B*
MATHEMATICS. *Arith.* *Algebra*	*Good work done. H.Mc.G* *Has worked well. F.Mc.G.*	
SCIENCE. *Geography* *Botany* **LANGUAGES.** *French*	*Good* *Improved* *Weak.*	*D.B* *D.B* *H.E.W*
MUSIC. *Singing*	*Fair*	*D.R.R*
DRAWING.	*Fairly Good*	*D.B*
Conduct *Good*		

Helen McGaffin
Principal.

Next Term commences on

Above: Abbey House, Abbey Foregate, 1906. A Grade II listed building from around 1710; Abbey House was the creation of Francis Smith of Warwick for his client Thomas Jenkins, who was later to become High Sheriff of Shropshire. Kinlet Hall and Davenport House are larger examples of Smith's draughtsmanship. It is an attractive brick-built town house with a multitude of windows to its six bay-front elevation. The interior contains a nice dogleg staircase with twisted balusters. It is hard to imagine but the property was originally the centre of an extensive estate; later in 1905 it was the town residence of Mary Frances Rouse Boughton of Downton Hall, Ludlow. Now in use as office accommodation, it was in the recent past used as a driving test centre.

Previous page below: Abbey House School, pupil's report. In 1930 the property was in use as a private boarding school for girls, the principal being Miss Helen McGaffin. The not too informative school report for pupil Nora Lee for the summer term bears witness to this fact. It is interesting to note that tuition, stationery and medical fees for this pupil for this particular term totalled £4 14d 6s.

Above, right: The Armoury, London Road, 1912. It is believed that the lady standing in front of her cottage is Mrs Minton with her child or grandchild. In this area between London Road and Wenlock Road were former military barracks, officer's quarters, a punishment block and workshops, plus an ammunition and explosives magazine – the Shrewsbury Armoury. Apart from a house and several cottages, little now remains. Part of the explanation is that after the 1914–18 war, Morris & Co. wished to develop their site in Victoria Avenue, Welsh Bridge. At this time building materials were in short supply and the Old Armoury/Barracks was purchased in order to provide the bricks for the construction of a bakery.

Right: St John's Military Hospital, Prestfelde, London Road, 1919. During the First World War this large private house was taken over by the Red Cross as a hospital for the treatment and care of servicemen wounded in the conflict. It closed its doors as a fifty-bed auxiliary hospital in March 1920. Here, the Earl of Powis pins the Royal Red Cross decoration on the uniform of the commandant of the hospital, Miss C.E. Hughes. At the time, only five such decorations had been awarded nationally. Miss Hughes had not been well enough to travel to London and Buckingham Palace to personally receive the honour from King George V.

Above and below: Nurses and patients at St John's Military Hospital, 1919. Prestfelde was built in around 1875 for Maj.-Gen. The Hon. W.H. Herbert, son of the Earl of Powis. After its exploits nursing military personnel, it opened as a school in 1930. It now forms part of the Woodard Foundation which encompasses many prominent public schools. This photograph taken in June 1919 and shows Miss M.B. Urwick, marked with a cross on the extreme left of the second row. The Revd Frederick Roberts, vicar of nearby St Giles, stands in the centre of the back row whilst Commandant Hughes sits centre stage on the front row. Sister Lewis and Miss Urwick sit with a variety of regimental patients including individuals from the Black Watch, Gordon Highlanders, the Dorset's, the Warwickshire's, the Yorkshire Regiment and the Army Service Corps. Miss Urwick was a sister of the well-known local medical consultant, Dr Urwick. She was an active lady in many charitable institutions including the Royal Orphanage at Wolverhampton.

British Fuel
for
British Transport

TOPHAM BROS (MANCHESTER) LIMITED.

The "Sentinel" Waggon Works, Ltd.,
Shrewsbury.

Above and below: Sentinel Wagon Works, Whitchurch Road. Heavy industry in the form of the Glasgow engineering firm Alley & MacLellan came to Shrewsbury in 1915. Amongst other things they were the manufacturers of steam wagons and were registered as Sentinel (Shrewsbury) Ltd. They were to provide work for 1,600 employees, together with extensive housing adjacent to the factory in Whitchurch Road. Heavy goods waggons, originally steam powered, were the end product. Diesel engines followed later. Starting in 1941, many changes in ownership were to take place, corresponding inevitably with product change and updating.

A Sentinel Standard flat-bed wagon from around 1921 stands outside the main entrance to the works. Although still on trade plates, the wagon is about to be delivered to W. Vernon & Sons of Seacombe, a subsidiary of the Spillers group of companies. No. 18 in their fleet, this particular firm is known to have purchased at least eight other Sentinel steam wagons.

This photograph is believed to show the first of only four Super Sentinel thirty-two seat buses to be produced by the Shrewsbury Works. Introduced in 1924, it failed to find a buyer in spite of extensive promotional outings. Introduced too late, its major design fault was the high floor level, which, in spite of a stepped platform, made access rather difficult. Registration NT 4950, shown here with solid tyres, was converted in 1925 to pneumatic type. Often used for staff outings, the remaining three buses were eventually sold abroad.

A local haulier, Richard M. Woolley of Bucknell, operated several Sentinel types until well after the Second World War. This vehicle is a Super Sentinel Double Geared Tractor, registration VN 4294, from 1949.

Atcham Bridge, 1929. Four bridges are known to have once crossed the Severn at this broad but shallow point. The last was erected by the County Council in 1929, replacing the adjacent and now preserved elegant structure of Grinshill freestone, designed by local architect John Gwynne and erected in 1776. This photograph shows a fleet of Sentinel steam wagons load testing the newly completed reinforced concrete bridge.

Shropshire Royal Horse Artillery, *c.* 1917. This unit of Shropshire gunners was to send two batteries to France and Flanders in the later stages of the First World War. The front line unit, lst/lst, served as 'A' Battery in 293 Brigade, RFA, whilst the second line unit, 2nd/1st, went as 'A' Battery, 158 Brigade, RFA. Other members of the unit – the Ammunition Column – saw service in the Trench Mortar Brigade, 58 London Division. The soldier in the centre of the back row wears a slouch hat, a left over from the Boer War.

No. 12800 Pte Alfred Richard Evans, 'C' Company, six 'old pals' Battalion KSLI. Private Evans, eldest son of Superintendent Alfred Evans of the Shropshire Constabulary, had previously worked for the Shropshire Co-operative Society before enlistment. Together with his brother, he arrived with his battalion in France in July 1915. In the following September he was engaged in the build-up to the Battle of Loos, where he sustained gunshot wounds inflicted by a sniper whilst his section were digging trenches and carrying forward supplies to the front line. He was later to die in a Field Hospital at the age of nineteen and is buried at Merville Communal Cemetery, near Lille. His brother, George, No. 12540, who was by his side when he fell, survived the conflict and went on to reach the rank of Inspector after twenty-seven' years service in the Shropshire Constabulary.

The Potts in a decrepit state, 1903. Taken on 24 June 1903, this snapshot shows an exploratory inspection taking place on the Shropshire and Montgomeryshire Railway between Ford Station and Shrawardine Viaduct. The photographer was F.E. Fox-Davies who is seated on the ganger's trolley at the front left, standing are Mr Reeves and G.M. Perkins, whilst seated alongside Fox-Davies is T.R. Perkins and Mr Morton. The line had not been used since 1880 and it was to be another eight years from this initial inspection before the line reopened on 13 April 1911 under the auspices of Colonel Stephens.

Shropshire and Montgomeryshire Railway, c. 1912. A train staff ticket signed by the stationmaster at Meole Brace authorising trains to proceed on the single line to Shrewsbury Abbey Foregate Station. Undated, this safety measure was likely to have been introduced during Coll Stephens' period in charge of operations, sometime after 1911.

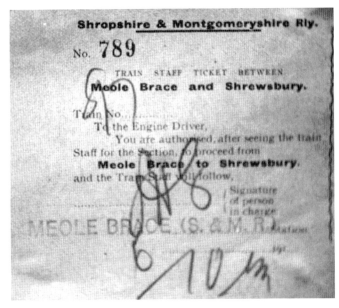

Meole Brace, Gallows Croft, 1931. This photograph, taken from the 'woody' bridge which connected Drawwell Street with Upper Hereford Road, shows Ceiriog stone-laden rail wagons from Criggion Quarry awaiting onward transmission through Shrewsbury over the national rail network. Exactly a decade later the War Department was to build more extensive transfer sidings a mile or so to the west at Red Hill/Hookagate. In a lane near here was once the site of a public gibbet, hence the name Gallows Croft; not now a nomenclature in common use.

Abbey Foregate Station, Shropshire and Montgomeryshire Railway, 5 August 1935. The hands of the clock on the Abbey Church approach 9.45 a.m. on a sunny August morning, and a special excursion begins to gather its passengers for the daytrip to Llanymynech and Criggion. The rear coach is rather special, being a former London and South Western Railway Royal saloon. Like the rest of the railway, this veteran was to suffer from a lack of care and, during the subsequent 'command' by the military, further neglect led to complete disintegration.

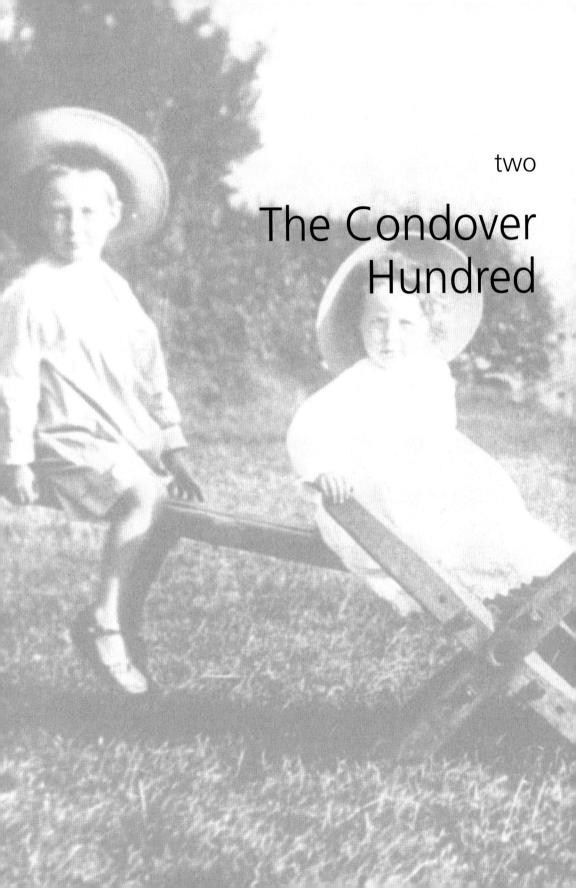

two

The Condover Hundred

Derivation of local place names:

Bayston Hill: A township meaning Beage Stone which refers to a rocky outcrop hereabouts.

Lyth Hill: From the Old English *hlith* which relates to the shape of the escarpment.

Condover: A name derivation from the nearby Cound Brook and the Old English *Ofer* meaning a bank. The Condor of Mary Webb.

Dorrington: Deritune at Domesday. Associated with Doda, a personal Saxon name. Dorinton from the seventeenth century.

Bayston Hill, 1931. The village Brownie pack is shown here outside the Memorial Hall with joint Brown Owls E.J.P. and B. Parry standing centre rear. Does anyone recognise themselves?

Opposite above: Lyth Hill Chapel, *c.* 1895. Always having strong connections with its sister chapel at Dorrington, this congregational chapel was built in 1795, the cost of which was largely borne by Sir Richard Hill of Hawstone, a strong supporter of Non-Conformism. Mainly due to its relative remoteness, the chapel was never known for large assemblies. It did, however, continue to function with various small improvements until the early 1930s. It is now converted to domestic use and virtually unrecognisable.

Opposite below: Spring Coppice, Lyth Hill, 1909. The three eldest children of William Owen and Janet Emily Wilding play on an improvised seesaw on a grassed area which seven years later was to become the garden of Spring Cottage and the home of novelist, Mary Webb. William Owen Wilding was the eldest son of Longworth Wilding, the founder of the stationery and printing business of that name at no. 33 Castle Street, Shrewsbury, from 1875 to 1982.

The Pye Pits, Condover, 1905. This area was so called because of clay extraction for pipe manufacture up until the middle of the nineteenth century. The timber-framed cruck construction Old School House was formerly a farmhouse and dates from the fifteenth century. The view down Station Road reveals the blacksmith's shop still in operation on the right, with an old Shropshire-style farm cart awaiting repair. The property has now been converted for domestic use and known appropriately as Farriers Cottage and the Old Smithy, the horse stocks remain amongst the trees.

Condover Post Office, 1905. Externally not a lot has changed since this date when Miss Catherine M. Millman was in residence as the sub-post mistress. Built in the early nineteenth century, this red brick house was later to be converted to retail use; it still retains its importance as a social meeting point, 100 years after this postcard was published. Its central trellis porch with long pointed finial, beneath a dummy window, has surprisingly not succumbed to modern thoughts. Smithy House on the right also survives and a ground floor extension is now in evidence to the left of the post office.

Condover House, 1906. Neddy waits patiently along a track just off the main road; which now forms the drive to Yew Tree Lodge. Placed at the lower end of the village, brick built Condover House is a former residence of the Dakin family and dates from the early eighteenth century. The finials to the roof dormers are distinctive as is the entrance porch of two storeys with its shaped gables. All are still extant. The building is currently in use by the Royal National Institute for the Blind as a Further Education Centre.

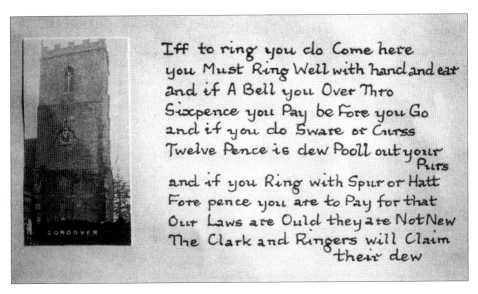

Iff to ring you do Come here
you Must Ring Well with hand and ear
and if A Bell you Over Thro
Sixpence you Pay be Fore you Go
and if you do Sware or Curss
Twelve Pence is dew Pooll out your Purs
and if you Ring with Spur or Hatt
Fore pence you are to Pay for that
Our Laws are Ould they are Not New
The Clark and Ringers will Claim their dew

St Mary & St Andrew, Condover. This little ditty bearing the date 1744 was found in the 1870s amongst other bell ringer's literature in the belfry of this late-Norman and thirteenth-century church. It is repeated here in its original form, the scribes spelling, turn of phrase and complete lack of punctuation adding to the overall effect.

47

Harper's Central Stores, Dorrington, 1913. Once a necessarily important social provision, village shops like this well-stocked store on the corner of Station Road have dwindled in number over recent years, due mainly to the advent of superstores. As was normal ninety years ago, these premises rendered an all-inclusive local service: grocer, baker, butcher, flour and corn merchant, as well as providing convenient post office facilities. Note the several flitches of bacon hanging on the shop wall above the delivery bicycle with its large front wicker basket. The Harper family, who lived next door at West View, ran their corner shop for many decades from around 1910. They also had farming interests locally.

Previous page top: Condover Hall and the Cound Brook, 1922. An unusual rear view of this fine local red sandstone Elizabethan mansion built for Thomas Owen and dated 1596. This view of the south west garden elevation illustrates the two projecting wings together with central arcade of nine bays. The RNIB moved here in 1946, however, its continued use as an education and care establishment is about to be terminated and the building sold, 2004.

Previous page below: Condover Railway Station, 1955. The provision of a railway connection in 1854 by the Shrewsbury and Hereford Company, albeit with a station a mile away from the village, must have made a significant impact on the villagers. At least some encouragement was given for them to travel further afield, not only for pleasure but also to provide an incentive for new and more varied employment. The bulk of the freight receipts were generated by local farmers, coal merchants Swain and Page, and, during the First World War, the airfield at Berriewood.

Dorrington Chapel, 1910. This congregational stronghold once bordered the main road through the village on the opposite corner to Harper's Stores. Built in 1808, it was later to benefit from the addition of a gallery in 1822 and further extensions in 1840 and 1868. Eventually, this was to prove to no avail for demolition came in the 1970s to cater for the advance of the motor car and the need for road widening and visibility improvements. Part of the burial ground survives.

Dorrington Village. This view looking south in the early 1950s has plenty of animation as villagers stop for a chat on their way to and from the post office and shops. Unthinkable now but here cars are parked on both sides of the road in what remains a rather restricted southern exit to the village. Whatever happened to the once-urgent notion that a bypass was needed here to help relieve this rural idyll of the plethora of through traffic?

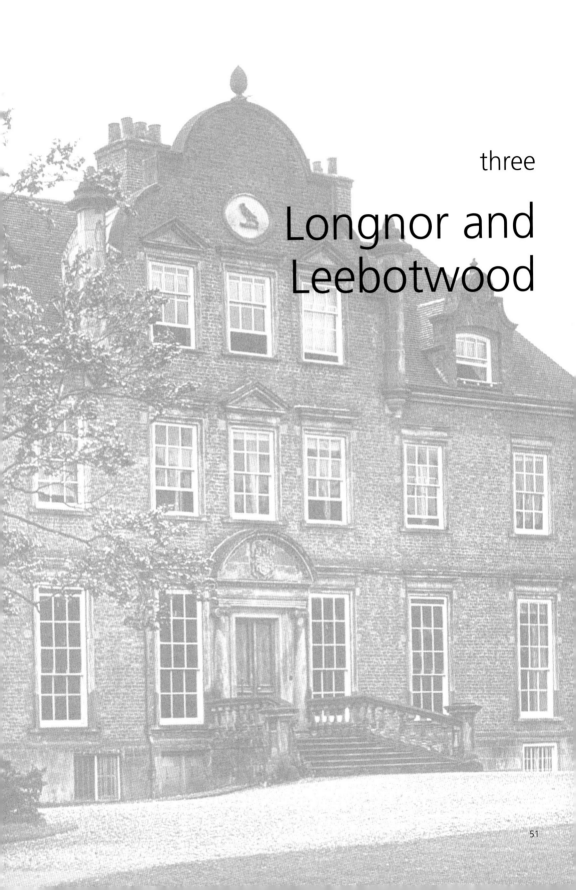

three

Longnor and Leebotwood

Derivation of local place names:

Longnor: Lege at Domesday, the parish name means 'a long alder copse'.

Leebotwood: Identified as a clearing in the wood belonging to Botta – a personal Saxon name.

Little Longnor, 1952. This hamlet is situated a little to the north of Longnor village on a minor road to Ryton and Condover which was once known as Lyde Way. Today, it is a cluster of dwellings around a ford on the Cound Brook. An iron furnace and forge were set up here by Richard Welbeck in 1605; reconstructed in around 1740, William Hazledine, the eminent local ironmaster, held the license here in the early days of the nineteenth century. He promptly converted the building into a paper mill. The lease was surrendered in 1815 and the mill closed down soon afterwards. The chimney illustrated is assumed to have been part of the old forge which, as Forge House, has been extensively modernised in recent times. Hereabouts the cottages were once occupied by colliers from the nearby Leebotwood Pit and later utilised for agricultural workers.

Micklewood, 1911. This house was built in 1680 for Watties Corbet, a member of the local landowning family. Placed a little away from Longnor village and close to the railway, the house has a nicely proportioned frontage of four bays, the middle two recessed; the central door case shows obvious signs of alteration. Having aged a little, the early Victorian dormers sit rather well in the hipped, tiled roofs. The property now functions as a farmhouse for the Thomas family.

The ford and footbridge, Longnor, 1912. This record of yesteryear clearly shows the old footbridge placed on its stone piers spanning the waters of the Cound Brook, together with sheep and cattle guards beneath. The large white-painted timbers are guide posts for horse-driven carts and the small number of cars likely to negotiate the ford in times of flood. The large block stone foundations of this footbridge remain in situ on the bed of the stream.

The ford, Longnor, 1920. Until 1925 villagers and visitors to Longnor, after leaving the main A49 Ludlow road, had to negotiate the vagaries of the Cound Brook; the situation would change quite dramatically following a thunderstorm over the Stretton Hills. The mill is shown in the background and the stream appears to be at summer drought level.

The New Bridge, Longnor. This picture shows the new bridge provided by the County Council in 1925. The design, an early example of the use of reinforced concrete in bridge construction, is of a type known as a multiple box culvert. It retains a pronounced hump especially when approached in haste!

Longnor corn and sawmill. Now much altered and largely converted to offices, this photograph of 1925 shows the nineteenth-century miller's house on the right, the timber-framed late seventeenth-century corn mill with its eaves level bag hoist at the centre, and the sawmill in the corrugated roof building to the front. All the machinery here was once driven by water from the nearby stream which had been diverted at a dam and sluice along a mill race flowing through the deer park and under the western boundary of the churchyard, to feed the two millponds and eventually the large wheel at side of the mill. The sawmill was a nineteenth century addition to the complex, the water-driven turbine would have provided the power to drive a confusing array of belts, cogs and pulleys. All milling activity here finished in 1934, the conversion of the machinery to electricity never being considered viable.

Longnor Hall, 1934. Hidden behind trees off the Shrewsbury to Ludlow road, the Corbett family mansion was completed in 1694 by Uvedale Corbett, his father, Sir Richard, having commenced the process a quarter of a century earlier. Of red brick with pale sandstone ashlar dressings, long sash windows, a central entrance with its eye-catching flight of steps and balustrade, all adding to the front elevations attractive symmetrical plan. The central gable, with Corbett raven emblem, effectively breaks up the roofline. Having been passed down, sometimes rather tenuously, through many generations of Corbett's over nearly three centuries, Longnor Hall was sold in 1949.

Longnor Hall. A football match is in progress at the rear of the Hall during the winter of 1940/1, when in use as a school. The lady writing this postcard on 11 January 1941 claims to be concerned for her own safety and that of the children. She states that 'there is a searchlight battery in one of the meadows nearby and that could be a target for the bombers.'

The Bank House, Longnor, 1910. Another Corbett Estate house. Still known locally as the Dower House, it was built in around 1755 but altered many times since, obviously not only to update things but also to suit the special needs of each generation. Historically, its location overlooking the main entrance to the village from the A49 would have been ideal for keeping a watchful eye on all employees and visitors alike!

Quality Row, Longnor, 1912. This charmingly named row of three cottages was surprisingly once a single dwelling. Much altered by the use of rendered brickwork to cover the timber frame and three cruck trusses. All this suggests they were built in the early sixteenth century.

Longnor School and School House, 1910. Situated on the approach road to the church of St Mary, the former village school dates from 1871, and enlarged in 1894. The schoolmasters' house to the left of the picture was initially pressed into use as teaching accommodation in the early years of the nineteenth century. A new school building was erected in 1957 a little higher up the village and now caters for over fifty pupils from a wide rural catchment area.

St Mary, Longnor, 1907. A delightful, unspoilt Early English church of 1260/70, situated on a slight ridge close to Longnor Hall, yet accessible for village folk. Once no more than a chapelry, probably of Condover, its interior is light, neat and still blessed with its Georgian west gallery and seventeenth- and eighteenth-century church furniture.

Above: The Grove Farm House, Longnor, on a postcard of 1909. Now used solely for domestic purposes and still part of the Corbett holdings, this building has a hidden timber frame of the late seventeenth century. The frontage is of rendered and painted brick with a neat Edwardian wrought-iron porch as a central feature. Edward Everall, the then tenant, may well be the gentleman at the front gate.

Left: Longnor village shop, 1905. A snapshot of Miss Alice Deakin, village shopkeeper and sub-post mistress standing at the entrance to her premises; she is accompanied by villagers and an array of various animals. The photograph is a little indistinct but the lady to the left appears to be carrying a bear cub!

Longnor village Post Office. On a postcard sent on 27 August 1911, Miss Alice Deakin, the sub-post mistress, poses for the camera outside her premises. Alice died on 17 December 1920 at the age of sixty-eight and is buried at St Mary's, Leebotwood. There was to be very little change back at the shop for Miss Alice Anna Deakin immediately took over the mantle and continued dispensing postal orders to villagers and sherbot suckers to the children until around 1947, when the little emporium was to close.

Longnor village shop and Post Office. Village children gather as an 8cwt Bull-Nose Morris makes
deliveries in early spring 1926. These properties, now known as Barset Cottage and Framley Cottage,
are of the mid-seventeenth century, timber-framed but with many twentieth-century alterations
and additions. The brick cottage to the left now has gabled eaves dormers and is painted white,
presumably to match its near neighbours.

Opposite above: Longnor, Stoneleigh. The village has a wealth of seventeenth-century timber-framed
cottages, most of which in the nineteenth century were occupied by miners and brickyard workers
employed locally at small scale workings associated with nearby Leebotwood and the southern
extremities of the Shrewsbury Coalfield. Known as Stoneleigh in 1910, when this postcard was
sent, the property has had numerous other titles in the intervening period but the local postman
now delivers to an unpretentious no. 12. The cottage has a nice integral brick chimney stack to the
South East elevation.

Opposite below: St Mary's, Leebotwood. This 1932 view by Mansells of Shrewsbury, does little to
highlight the imaginative placement of this church on rising ground above the railway, but a little
away from its present flock. As at nearby Smethcott, the village originally surrounded the church
at the higher level. St Mary's is rather simple in design, rectangular, under one continuous roof,
the west tower and present entrance being added in 1829. The presence here of Early English wall
paintings was discovered in 1976.

Cardington Road, Leebotwood, 1932. Turning off the Shrewsbury to Ludlow road, the narrow lanes rise steadily to join Old Watling Street and reach a zenith near Comley, high up between the Lawley and Caer Caradoc. On the left is Smithy Cottage, the Smithy – the stone building alongside – was demolished in 1963, not having been in use since 1939. Outside Horseshoe Farm on the right, once an ale house and now resplendent with a new porch, is parked a little buggy with a dickey seat. Both properties have now cast-off their careworn look of seventy years ago, whilst the long barn to the rear now caters for mere mortals rather than livestock.

Previous page top: The Pound Inn, Leebotwood, 1934. This photograph shows Kathleen and Margaret Beamond, whose family were from the Longmynd in the Gogbatch and Inwood area, posing for the camera outside the village shop which just happened to be managed at this time by Samuel Beamond and his wife, Ruth. Perhaps the children had popped over to see grandma and grandpa?

Previous page below: Heather Brae garage, Leebotwood, 1910. It is difficult to correlate this scene with the present day rural crafts centre, the interim period having seen the demise of this once busy garage and petrol filling station. The main A49 trunk road here has also been improved since this date, coinciding with a considerable increase in traffic.

The Brownhills, Leebotwood. Situated across fields opposite where the Heather Brae garage once stood and eastwards towards the Lawley, Brownhills is a large farmhouse of around 1830. Recently modernised, a visitor to the property in the summer of 1908 wrote a postcard home to Bootle on Merseyside saying 'how pleasant things were but he was excusing himself from going up the hill as it was raining hopelessly'.

Leebotwood, Pensylvania. This 1908 view shows an intriguingly named small country house situated on a minor road between Lower Wood and Dudgeley. The decorative barge boards to the gable and the leaded lights to the windows give no indication as to why this house was so named. The Keystone State, a major battleground during the American Civil War might provide a hidden clue!

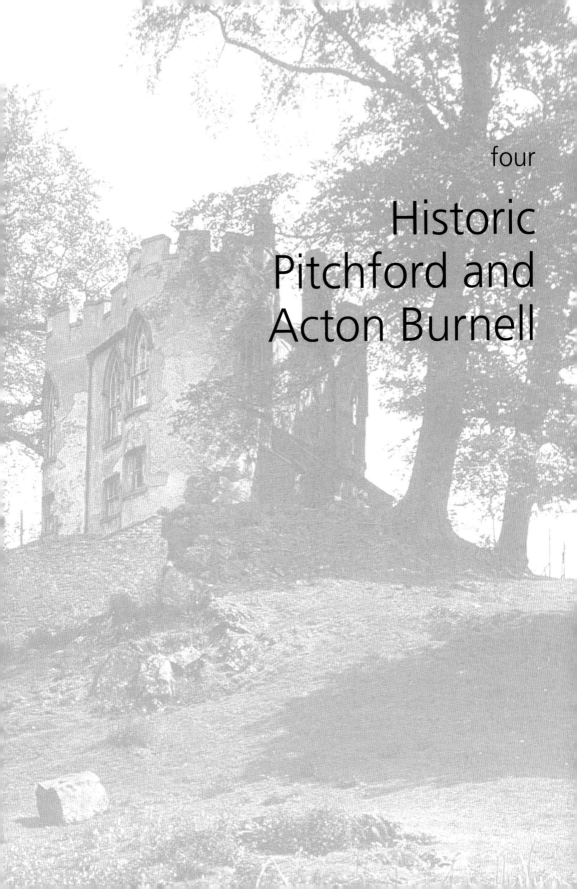

four

Historic
Pitchford and
Acton Burnell

Derivation of local place names:

Pitchford: Named after a pitch well near a ford on the Row Brook.

Acton Burnell: An oak settlement and home of the Burnell family.

This is an area steeped in history. A Roman road divides the parishes, one of which, Pitchford, boasts an outstanding mid-sixteenth-century half-timbered mansion erected on behalf of the Ottley family, wealthy Shrewsbury wool merchants. Acton Burrell, once a parliamentary meeting place, openly beckons visitors to its twelfth-century ruined fortified manor house and church of St Mary.

St Michael and All Angels, Pitchford. Everything appears to be well-maintained would be the obvious comment when attempting to describe this vista from the drive to Pitchford Hall. St Michael's, which continues in its role as a small parish church, has in more recent times suffered from restricted access. This is a great pity because it exudes rural charm, allied to its Norman foundation, complete with lancet windows and herringbone masonry. A small church with much thirteenth- and fourteenth-century work to see.

The Tree House, Pitchford Hall. A carte de visite of 1869. The story is that this substantial structure within the branches of a large spreading lime tree in the grounds of the Hall was built for the Hon. Charles Jenkinson, later the 3rd Earl of Liverpool. He was MP for Bridgnorth and died in 1851. Its purpose – a smoking parlour! However, its building date is more likely to be 1720-40. The tree house is a listed structure, like the main building, the whole being of the highest architectural and historical importance.

The Tree House interior, 1922. This was no ordinary smoking parlour as can be seen by the Rococo Gothic plasterwork to its interior. Princess Victoria, as a young teenager, visited Shrewsbury on 2 August 1832; she stayed at Pitchford with her mother, the Duchess of Kent, and apparently was entranced with the charm and originality of the tree house. It was also the favourite spot of the eccentric Lady Sybil Grant, daughter of the 5th Earl Rosebery and the wife of General Sir Charles Grant. She died in 1955 and loved to spend summer nights amongst the branches.

Christmas

Pitchford Hall Shropshire.

1907

Acton Burnell stores and Post Office, 1912. By 1870 this property, together with the adjoining two houses, had been much altered to form the Stags Head Inn with Miss Matilda Southern filling the jugs. Immediately adjacent, as shown on the photograph, was Thomas Peate Perks' rural bazaar which also included a tea shop. Lady Smythe and her 'companion' stand at the entrance. Ernest Stockton, baker and confectioner, joined the business in 1916 and stayed for over fifty years, living across the road at no. 19. Thomas Perks died in 1942, age sixty-nine, and is buried in the parish churchyard.

Previous page top: Pitchford Hall entrance porch, 1920. This close-up view shows the seventeenth-century louvered bellcote and clock within the shaped gable to the south porch, with much fine detailing. This is an outstanding example of sixteenth-century timber-framing on a large scale. The national treasure is privately owned and unfortunately there is some danger of deterioration.

Previous page below: Pitchford Hall, family Christmas card. Seasonal greetings were sent by Lt-Col. Charles James Cotes and his family in 1907. Colonel Coates was a direct descendent of the Jenkinsons, Earl's of Liverpool, the 2nd Earl being Prime Minister from 1812-27. A later descendant, General Sir Charles Grant, was to marry Lady Primrose, daughter of another Prime Minister, the 5th Earl Rosebery.

Above: Acton Burnell Hall, 1910. Situated in extensive parkland with numerous mature cedars, lakes and tree-covered hill, the Hall was the home of the Smythe's for several centuries. Of the Roman Catholic faith, the family originated from Durham and through the marriage of Edward Smythe to Mary, heiress daughter of Sir Richard Lee (d.1660), came into possession of the Acton Burnell estate. The Hall, a large neo-Classical style building of 1814 by John Tasker, is of stuccoed ashlar with a significant Ionic portico. In recent times it has been in use as a convent school but the Concorde College now caters for students from the Far East, and a considerable number of new buildings have been erected in the grounds.

Acton Burnell Cricket Team, *c.* 1930. A team of novices when they first started in 1920, they were eventually to establish themselves as one of the better village teams in Shropshire. They played on the Hall Meadow on a very attractive tree-surrounded oval ground in front of the Hall and their players included some from the neighbouring villages of Pitchford, Cantlop and Kenley. The team regularly included up to seven Edwards's – all related. The club secretary and team member for many years was Ernest Stockton, baker at the village stores. The club was reformed after Second World War but lasted only a few seasons. The youngsters of the area attempted a revival in the 1950s but it did not gain sufficient impetus to succeed. Those in the photograph include, from left to right back row: Mr Howlett (senior), Ernest Stockton, Bert Hancocks, Douglas Edwards, Angus McDonald, Albert Howlett. Front row: Bill Preece (scorer), Percy Edwards, Charlie Edwards, Sid Edwards, Tom 'Rabbit' Edwards.

Opposite: Fire at Acton Burnell Hall. On Tuesday 14 April 1914 a serious fire almost completely destroyed Sir Walter Smythe's residence resulting in damage estimated at £35,000. This view shows the extent of the destruction. The fire was detected at midday in Lady Smythe's bedroom; she had been confined to her bed for the previous three weeks and part of the palliative remedy was a constant fire in this room. The result was an igniting of an oak beam in the roof void. The fire, rapidly spread by a strong wind, was first tackled by the personal fire-fighters of Alexander Cowan McCorquodale from Cound Hall, later joined by steam appliances from Shrewsbury and Wellington. Three hours later, in mid-afternoon, the fire had been extinguished but the building was a skeleton. However, valuable furniture and pictures were saved, together with estate plans and deeds, but silver and Venetian glass was lost, together with a library of books.

Coronation celebrations, Acton Burnell, 1911. Most villages in the county held festivities to celebrate the Coronation of King George V and Queen Mary on 11 June 1911. At Acton Burnell a special service was held at the parish church, followed by lunch for the farming fraternity and tea for the women and children in Mr Morgan Jones' Dutch barn at Home Farm. Sports and games were organised for the afternoon on the field opposite Acton Burnell Farm. The children were presented with commemorative mugs and a band accompanied communal dancing. The climax appears to have been an evening bonfire and fireworks display, all of which took place on the topmost field of the park. A picture similar to this rather faded example appeared in the *Shrewsbury Chronicle* on 7 July, when the bonfire was described as being made of birch wood faggots and brushwood, 60 yards in circumference and reaching a height of 45ft.

A mid-1930s postcard of Acton Burnell Castle. Steeped in history, Robert Burnell's fortified manor house of 1285 stands centre stage with its battlemented parapets and projecting square towers of grey and red local sandstone. Used as a barn in the eighteenth century, roofs were added later that century over the south-west tower and west block. Burnell was Chancellor of England and Bishop of Bath and Wells in the reign of Edward I. St Mary's parish church, which is contemporary with the castle, stands to the left whilst the Hall is to the right. Out of shot and further to the east stand the gable ends of a large thirteenth-century stone barn, often erroneously referred to as the Parliament Barn.

Keeper's House, Acton Burnell Park, 1928. Often described as a sham castle and a folly, it was built in 1780 as a prospect tower by Samuel Scoltock, a Shrewsbury artisan who died in 1819 and is buried at the Abbey Church. Castellated and triangular in plan with circular towers at each corner, it is of red brick and cement-rendered and sits on a part wooded eminence overlooking the Lower or Shadwell Pool. Badly neglected and vandalised, with staircases and eighteenth-century fireplaces removed, the building was restored to something like its previous grandeur by a local businessman in the 1970s.

The Crossroads (1), Acton Burnell, 1910. Nearing the top of the village and looking down towards Pitchford and Shrewsbury. Weeds grow in the gutter and there is plenty of evidence that horses or cattle recently passed this way. All these cottages survive; no.16 on the immediate left was the sub-post office for many years last century. New housing now proliferates on both sides of the road but everything still remains rather homely.

The Crossroads (2), Acton Burnell, 1932. The photographer stands in Hall Road in the heart of the village looking towards Frodesley and the Roman road which once led from Wroxeter southwards towards Leintwardine (*Bravonium*) and Caerleon in South Wales.

Frodesley Road, Acton Burnell. Looking back towards the crossroads, this view is also dated 1932. The old village school, built in 1815 and twice enlarged, is shown on the right; it was closed in the 1970s, a fate soon to overcome its successor built at the top of the village on the road to Langley. Here children gather outside the 1920s-built agricultural workers cottages and on the stile and wall opposite.

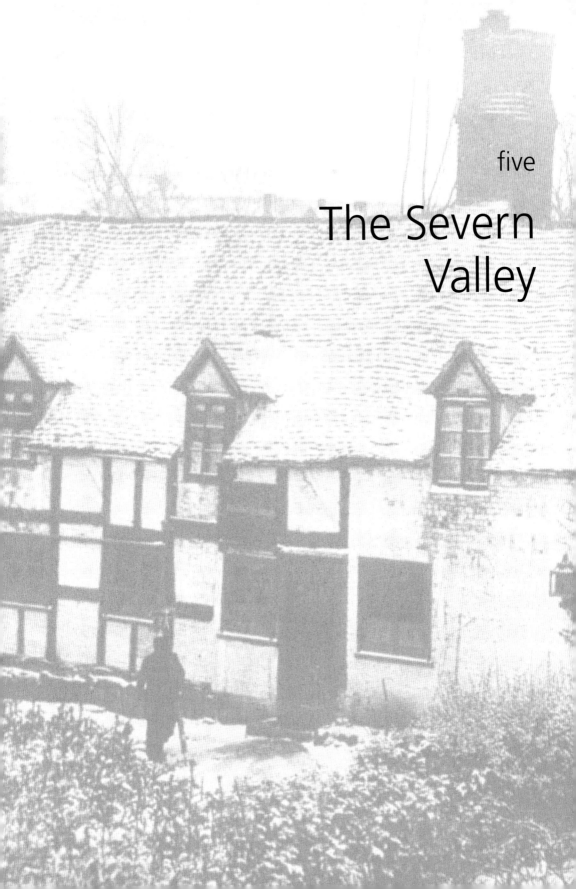

five

The Severn Valley

Derivation of local place names:

Betton Strange: Derived from the Old English *Bectun*; a beech tree. The 'Strange' element being from a family of that name who held the manor in the twelfth century.

Berrington: Old English *Byrhtun*; an ancient settlement associated with a fortification.

Cross Houses: A seventeenth-century crossroads squatter settlement.

Cound: Of Celtic roots and linked to Cound Brook.

Cressage: From Saxon *Christache* meaning Christ's Oak.

Harley: Harlege at Doomsday. Derivation likely from *haer*; stony or rocky escarpment with a clearing – a 'leah'.

Kenley: Meaning Cena's (personal name) clearing.

Sheinton: From Anglo-Saxon *Sciene* or *Scyne*, meaning a beautiful or fair place in an open position.

Buildwas: From Middle English (twelfth- to fourteenth-century) *bilde* and Anglo Saxon *Waes*, hence a building in the marsh or bog.

Betton Strange, 1916. Like other large houses throughout the county, Betton Strange was requisitioned for military use as a Voluntary Aid Hospital during the First World War. A Model T Ford ambulance awaits its next duty outside the Tuscan colonnaded frontage. Two-thousand six-hundred and forty-five of these early Ford vehicles were turned out by the production line at Trafford Park, Manchester, between 1915 and 1919. The Scott family were lords of the manor here for over 300 years and they were responsible for building this mid-nineteenth century country house in a Queen Anne Revival style. The whole is stuccoed and painted and now converted into flats.

Berrington Station, 1912. Situated between Berrington and Cross Houses villages, this was the first station out of Shrewsbury on the Severn Valley Branch line to Bridgnorth, Kidderminster and Hartlebury. During the war years considerable freight traffic was generated by the RAF and later, in mid-1942, by the USAF, both based at Atcham airfield. Apart from reasonable usage by passengers, there was regular trade in agricultural-based products including basic slag, fertilisers, animal foods, potatoes and sugar beet; the latter destined for Allscott Beet Factory, Walcot. The station closed to passengers in 1965 and the whole line a little later after the transportation of engineering equipment to Buildwas Power Station.

Berrington Station staff, 1943. This photograph, taken in the station yard near to the weighbridge, shows the staff responsible for the running of the station in wartime conditions. Eileen Barber, a Birmingham lass, later in 1947 to become Mrs Owen, was an essential cog in this small operation. She was the booking clerk and universally referred to by the male staff as 'the princess'. Porter Edward Peters of Bayston Hill is on the left whilst the two railwaymen on the right are Richard Furber, signalman, of Trinity Street, Shrewsbury, and lorry driver Percy Painter of Pitchford. The name of the station master with the 'scrambled egg' on his hat is not known.

Cross Houses.

The village shop, Cross Houses, 1905. Thomas Heighway was then the proprietor of these premises. In addition to general groceries and provisions, he also had extensive interests as a merchant dealing in flour, bran and meal – note the bag hoist to the right of the photograph. The perambulator is something special! The postcard was sent by Willie Heighway, a son of Thomas, to his granny, Mrs Charlotte Heighway, at Sibberscote, Lea Cross, Pontesbury. Walter Lindop ran the business between the two world wars and trading continues today, the shop now doubles up as the sub-post office.

Previous page top: Berrington Hall and Rectory, 1906. Formerly the rectory, this small country house of 1805 was built to a design by Joseph Bromfield of Shrewsbury, on behalf of The Hon. Revd Richard Noel Hill, a member of nearby Attingham's Berwick family. The centrally placed Tuscan-columned porch to the west-facing front of five bays provides a neat example of architecture of the period. It is assumed that the stables and carriage facilities lay at a much lower level across fields to the north east at what is now referred to as Berrington Barns, a property which was once owned by the Berwick's and later the National Trust.

Previous page below: Cross Houses village. With the photographer facing towards Shrewsbury this scene shows the village street as it was in 1925. The brick, gabled house to the left had yet to burgeon into an important retail store and tea rooms. The sub-post office is on the right. All the white-painted cottages to the left of the picture have been lost to road improvements and the versatile and durable Model T Ford delivery vans have long found their way to the scrap yard.

Cound Primary School, *c.* 1930. Placed on glebe land opposite the church, the village school was opened in 1844, the building and equipment costs being met by Mrs Frances Thursby, the widow of the Revd G.A. Thursby, a former rector. A schoolmaster's house was also built, the property remaining in the hands of the church that supported its upkeep and at the same time levying a small graduated 'school pence' fee which was finally abolished in 1892. Government grants were forthcoming from 1870, supported by a voluntary school rate. Attendance figures fluctuated greatly, reaching a peak of just over 100 in 1902, which made it necessary to move the infant children across the road to the nearby Guildhall. Only sixteen children were on the school roll when closure came in 1963. The identities of the children in the photograph are not known but hopefully a reader may be able to help provide some of their names?

Previous page top: Cross House village, *c.* 1938. This view from what was then a lane leading to Brompton shows the Misses Edith and Minnie Machin's tea rooms and shop on the main A458 road through the village. The Methodist chapel is shown on the right. Both properties are no longer used for such purposes, reverting to domestic use. The road now provides access to new housing development including council houses. The grassed 'island' at the T-junction has long since gone.

Previous page below: Cound Rectory, 1906. Overlooking the cricket field and adjacent to the Guildhall and St Peter's, the rectory, with its fine views of the Wrekin, was the usual site for the annual church and village school fêtes. Many a time was the author all but 'caught out' in the 1960s fielding on the boundary whilst at the same time holding a learned conversation with the then rector, the Revd Sidney Evans, as he leaned on the iron hurdle perimeter fencing.

Cound Cricket Club, *c.* 1952. As an ex-club member this photograph is full of nostalgia but tinged with sadness, for most of those pictured have since passed away. Amongst the cricketers shown are Derrick Donnell, Clarrie Woodhouse, Reg Purslow, Arthur Meredith, and Jim Whittingham. Megan Donnell is the lady scorer.

Cound Halt, 1952. Placed immediately behind the former Cound Lodge Inn, the temporary-looking wooden platform and passenger shelter never did achieve any permanency. After all, the likely ticket sales based on the neighbourhood population must always have been negligible. Tickets to travellers were issued on the train by the booking clerk at Berrington or Cressage, depending on the journey direction.

Cound Hall laundry, 1909. Laundresses stand outside the newly-built laundry block in the lane opposite the Cound Lodge Inn. Situated one mile distant from Cound Hall, the building was provided by the then squire, Alexander Cowan McCorquodale, a fact commemorated on the plaque above the front doorway. Mr McCorquodale died in 1941 and the estate broken up and sold.

War Memorial, Cressage. This 1930 postcard shows the stone cross at the main road intersection, the cost of erection being by public subscription, in memory of the men of Cressage who gave their lives in the Great War, 1914-18. Seventeenth-century Fingerpost Cottage stands in the background. The uniformed gentleman is a bit of a mystery. A speculative guess might be that he is a lookout linesman from the nearby Great Western Railway line, as he appears to be carrying rolled-up signalling flags together with a warning horn.

The Crown Inn, Cressage, 1906. Formerly a farmhouse, the Crown probably dates from the early days of the seventeenth century. Situated in a quiet spot off the busy A458, it is a timber-framed building of some interest. With a large rear stack, roof dormers and painted brick infill, it now makes an attractive sympathetically restored private house. The interior displays a fully exposed frame and champfered spine beam. It must have been a rather busy place 100 years ago when Richard Reynolds was licensee. Footpaths led across the fields, then known as 'yards', from Wood Lane and the main road next to the post office. It was certainly a favourite rendezvous for children, for it was here that they obtained their sherbet suckers and home-made ginger beer from a lean-to shop then attached to the Malthouse adjacent to the Crown. The Malthouse building itself was regularly used for dancing classes during and after First World War. From around 1930 the complex of buildings was owned by Clough Williams Ellis of Portmeirion fame and it was he who purchased the Mytton and Mermaid at Atcham from the Attingham Estate and turned it back into a reputable hotel, transferring the necessary licence from the Crown Inn in 1932.

The village shop and church in Harley Road, Cressage, 1923. This postcard was sent as a New Year card and the sender, Bert, is very likely to have been Herbert Brown, painter and decorator, whose advertising sign is displayed on the walls of his shop. Christ Church, a former chapelry of nearby Cound, was erected in 1841 in the Early English Style by local architect Edward Haycock. The former church of St Sampson, an unusual dedication, was placed on the river flood plain near to the old railway line.

Cressage School, 1906. Situated on the Harley Road opposite the church, this National School was erected in 1857. Under church guidance, it was greatly enlarged and remodelled in 1872 under the direction of architect, Richard Norman Shaw. Government grant aid was to eventually supplant all other sources of support and the small school serving fifty pupils achieved controlled status in 1955. The building is now a private dwelling, the pupils having transferred to a new and much larger school off Sheinton Road, which caters for a wider catchment area and a significantly increased village population.

The Green, Harley, 1910. Long since bypassed by the busy A458, the village remains a rather tranquil place, apparently undisturbed by the urgency of modern life. By way of contrast, from medieval times limestone was extracted hereabouts for firing in local kilns, as was clay for small local brickworks. A smithy, opposite the old school, operated until 1944 and shoemakers, carpenters, stonemasons, bricklayers and a wheelwright, are all recorded as being once essential elements of the local economy. Additionally, an iron forge was in operation until the seventeenth century and a water mill on the Harley Brook did not close until 1905. The dwellings on the right-hand side of the photograph have all been demolished, making way for modern development set back further from the highway. The white-painted building in the distance was formerly part of the Unicorn Inn which closed in around 1870.

Harley Cottages and church 1906. The village is prominently placed at the north east end of a long rocky ridge running from Enchmarsh through Chatwall and Kenley. St Mary's sixteenth-century west tower, crenellated and with pyramidal roof, here stands aloft between Church Cottage (formerly Old Timbers) and no. 3 Harley. Church Cottage is timber-framed but now encased in stone, whilst no. 3 is an outstanding example of a sixteenth-century yeoman's dwelling. Although recently extended laterally in red brick, it has a Queen Post roof construction amongst nicely exposed timbers. Miss Frances Pitt, local naturalist and author, resided with her menagerie at Castle Hill House (of 1840) for many decades after Second World War. The oldest house in the village is the fifteenth-century Old Rectory with prominent Georgian extension.

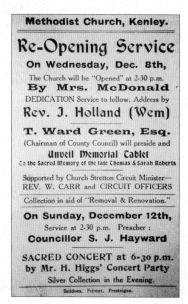

Kenley Methodist Chapel. An important milestone for non-conformists in this area was the re-opening in 1936 of a re-sited and newly refurbished Methodist chapel at Kenley Common. The chapel, which was little more than a tin shack, had previously been placed near Bull Farm. However, custom did not proliferate and the chapel closed many decades ago and was demolished in around 1975.

Right: Sheinton village, 1906. This view of the church and centre of the village from a high vantage point shows the congregation gathered at the roadside in their broughams and pony and traps. Cars and tractors now negotiate these narrow lanes, otherwise little appears to have changed in the intervening 100 years.

Below: Sheinton Parish Church, 1906. Superbly positioned on a wooded ridge overlooking the water meadows of the Severn, the church of St Peter and St Paul has over many centuries been subject to extensive rebuilding and restoration and much of what is left is of the nineteenth century. However, externally the half-timbered pyramidal bell turret is of some antiquity, charmingly capped by an old-world weathercock. The register only dates from 1711, the earlier elements having long been mislaid.

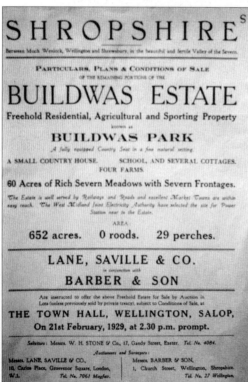

Above: Buildwas Park, *c.* 1912. This country house of an Elizabethan Gothic style was built for Walter Moseley in 1830 on a near perfect site overlooking the meandering River Severn and facing north towards the Wrekin. The frontage is shown here when the tenant was Samuel Sandbach Parker JP. It is assumed that the picture shows some of the servants, having discarded their bicycles, quietly relaxing on the lawn.

Left: Buildwas Estate sale. The break-up of this centuries-old estate took place on 21 February 1929. The existing tenant of the house and its immediate surrounds, a Colonel Crichton-Browne, was successful in purchasing this element – Lot no. 13. Later, during the 1939/45 war, the house was requisitioned by the military and used by USAF personnel stationed at Atcham airfield. Considerable damage was caused to the fabric and the house does not appear to have been lived in again. It was demolished in 1957.

six

Allscott and Admaston

Derivation of local place names:

Allscott: Formerly Aldredescote and Aldescote and part of Wrockwardine Manor. Derivation from Ealdred's (Aldred's) Cottages.

Admaston: Previously known as Ademoneston, the meaning derived from Aedelmund's (Edmund's) estate or homestead.

Very much part of Wrockwardine St Peter's parish flock, the two villages of Allscott and Admaston are neighbours of contrast. Different in size, rural Allscott has benefitted from selective small-scale development. Conversely, enlarged urban Admaston is now part of the all-embracing philosophy of the New Town of Telford.

The Grove Hotel, Walcot. The frontage of the Grove has changed little since this postcard was published in 1914. This former railway hotel, built in the mid-nineteenth century, is of red brick and still retains its ornate barge boards and small pane bay windows. The touch of convenience with the local post box set in the wall at this crossroads location has long since gone, as has the hotel's first floor veranda. Any custom generated by the nearby railway station was extinguished with the removal of stopping trains in the 1960s.

Allscott Beet Factory. This photograph shows the first buildings being erected on behalf of the Shropshire Beet Sugar Co. Ltd in November 1927. Deliberately positioned at the centre of the county, with a rail connection, most beet was initially grown within fifteen miles of the factory, although 26 per cent was more than twenty-five miles distant. There were 1,500 farmer growers by 1938. In the first years of the 1950s the British Sugar Corporation undertook an extensive redevelopment programme, the result being the on-site completion of the full refining process. Table sugar thus being produced from beet on this one site!

GREAT WESTERN RAILWAY.

OWNER & NO. OF WAGON _____ DATE _____ 19___

SUGAR BEET URGENT

From_____

To ALLSCOTT (Beet Factory) SIDING, G.W.R.

Consignee—
BRITISH SUGAR CORPORATION, LTD.
(ALLSCOTT FACTORY)
Contract No._____

Senders Full Name_____
12,000 12/44.

Allscott Beet Factory, railway freight label. This Great Western Railway wagon label of the 1930s does, if nothing else proves that at that time not all sugar beet was delivered by steam wagon, lorry or horse and cart. Seventy years ago most country railway stations in central Shropshire had sidings facilities enabling local farmers to send their beet crops to Allscott by the wagon load.

Allscott Beet Factory, 1928/9. A Super Sentinel three-way tipper steam wagon, registration NT 9922, simmers away as its load of sugar beet is delivered into the factory hoppers. Owned by S.J. Hayward & Co. Ltd, this wagon was no. 20 in their mixed fleet of lorries and wagons; it still retains its solid tyres and acetylene side lamps. The Hayward Company had its registered offices at Talbot Chambers, Market Street, Shrewsbury, but the essential nuts and bolts of the Hayward business emanated from the Severn House Garage at Montford Bridge, where all vehicles were garaged, serviced and repaired.

Allscott Beet Factory, 1928/29. S.J. Hayward & Co. Ltd, Montford Bridge and Shrewsbury, haulage contractors, took delivery of three Super Sentinel three-way tippers in 1927 – shown here in a promotional photograph. There appears to be numerous officials posing for the camera, presumably from the Sentinel Wagon Works, the contractors, Hayward, and the Sugar Beet Factory, and there appears to be little interest in the actual simultaneous entry of beet into the hoppers.

Number 7, Allscott. This seventeenth-century listed timber-framed cottage is now in the throws of modernisation and virtually unrecognisable when compared with this family photograph of 1930. Here, Mrs Alice Rogers (*née* Grainger) stands in the front garden holding the hands of her nieces Kathleen and Joyce Rivett, her sister Jessie's children. Family tragedy was to follow a few years later when Kathleen was killed in a road accident whilst cycling not 100 yards from the cottage near the Plough Inn.

Numbers 7 and 8, Arscott. Godfrey Rogers poses with a child in his Bullnose Morris in 1928. Margaret Grainger, who later became Mrs Minor, is the lady on the left leaning on the gate of no. 7. No. 8, the cottage to the left, was the home of Reginald and Annie Minor; the identities of the lady in the doorway and the young child are not known.

Wrockwardine, 1927. Mr Godfrey Rogers on a visit to relatives at the nearby hamlet of Aston, near Wrockwardine, poses astride his Shropshire New Imperial motorcycle, registration NT 4850. One of his nieces is believed to be riding pillion.

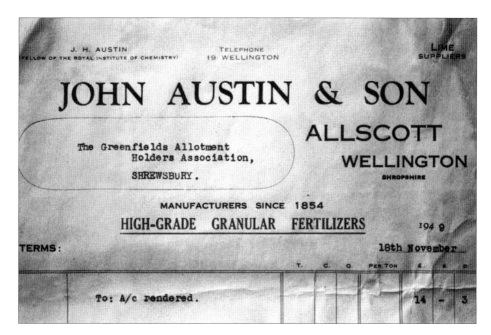

John Austin & Son, Allscott. This billhead of 1949 was sent to the Greenfields Allotment Holders Association in Shrewsbury for the supply of bagged fertilizers. John Austin specifically dealt in bulk with this commodity as well as limestone and other agricultural necessities. Mr Austin and his family lived in an attractive nineteenth-century residence, the Manor House, just a short distance away in Allscott village itself.

Admaston Spa and the Clock house. The first-known reference to mineral springs here was in 1764, becoming well-established by the late eighteenth and early nineteenth century. The waters were comparable to those at Harrogate, being chalybeate saline by analysis. The sulphur rich springs were particularly popular with the Victorians. The Clock house is a Grade II listed building of 1840, stuccoed with a low-pitch hipped slate roof which, over the years has been subject to numerous additions.

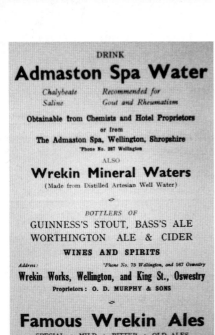

Left: Admaston Spa Water advertisement. This 1933 advertisement does its best to extol the many virtues of this local spa water. It had by this time been brought under the aegis of O.D. Murphy and the Wrekin Brewery Company. As the wording suggests, the partaking of the waters may well go someway towards combating the side effects of one of their other products – alcohol.

Below: Admaston Smithy, 1912. A local farmer holds his horse steady as the farrier, John Marsh, prepares to carry out re-shoeing work. The smithy, long reduced to rubble, was situated near the crossroads in the centre of the village and next to the gardener's cottage of nearby Admaston Hall.

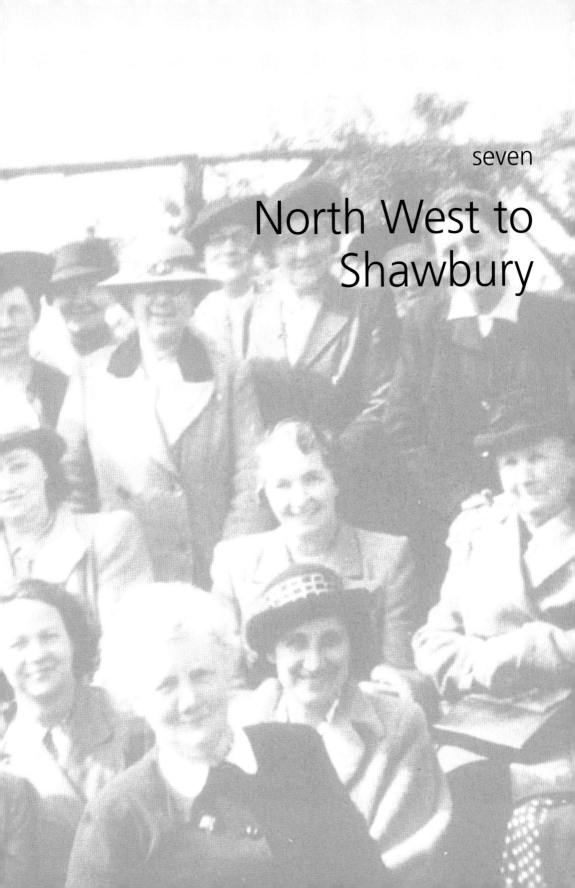

seven

North West to Shawbury

Derivation of local place names:

Albright Hussey: From a common Saxon name, *Eadbeorht*. The Hussey family held it after Domesday.

Astley: Literal meaning 'an eastside clearing in a wood once stretching to the River Severn.'

Hadnall: Hadehelle at Domesday and possibly, derived from Old English personal name of *Headda*.

Shawbury: An ancient parish, originally Sawesberie, meaning a manor house by a small wood.

Stanton: Derived from the Old English 'a stone settlement'.

Ellerdine: Simply meaning 'Ella's settlement.'

Roden: Originates from the Romano-British *Rutunium*, meaning a swift flowing river.

High Ercall: An ancient parish, formerly *Arcalum/Earcaluw* and meaning low hill from Old English. 'High' element synonymous with great or magna.

Albright Hussey, 1908. Situated very close to the area of conflict at the Battle of Shrewsbury, 1403, this half-and-half manor house is now in use as a restaurant. The timber-framed portion of 1524 with its diagonal struts and lozenges acts as a perfect foil to its neighbour of brick and stone dressings of 1601. The whole paints a delightful picture, there being every possibility that the black and white element only remains because of an unachieved second phase of a complete rebuilding.

Astley House, 1930. A three-storey imposing country mansion, not surprisingly listed as being of some architectural interest. It is a later remodelling (1830) of an earlier Georgian house. Perhaps rather over-fussy, the Greek Revivalist style seems out of place in a country setting. The Doric-columned entrance porch, the colonnade and the numerous full length pilasters are all stucco rendered and paint finished. Members of' the Philip family lived here a century ago and their keen interest in horse training and dealing must have had a considerable impact on life in the village of Astley.

Astley Remount Depot, 1915. Two members of the Philip family, Walter and Percy, were living at this time in two large houses in Astley – the Firs and Astley House. Both of these gentlemen described themselves as horse dealers and their transactions were largely with the military. Such activities required extensive stabling facilities and it is known that one such establishment was at the Firs. This was primarily a Remount Depot where horses were accepted for breaking in; taught to accept a saddle and bridle and eventually a rider. Such animals were accepted for military service where they first had to get used to the proximity of small arms and gun fire. Thousands, if not millions of these horses joined the various army corps and cavalry regiments to see service transporting men, supplies, ammunition and artillery around the First World War battlefields. Most of the work at these training depots was carried out by civilians. It is believed that local man, Ned Tomlins, is one of those pictured.

Left: Ivy Cottage, no. 26 Shrewsbury Road, Hadnall, *c.* 1928. The lady leaning on her garden gate is Mary Ellen Jones who had taken on the tenancy of the property with her husband, John, in 1899. They had many children including Jack, Emily, Nelly, Agnes, Fred, Bert and William. This postcard was sent to a relative in Birkenhead by Mary Ellen passing on some news about Tom and Charlie!

Below: Ladymas Corner, Hadnall. This posed photograph published in 1917 depicts the turn off from the A49 towards Sansaw, Black Birches and Harmer Hill. The term Ladymas is thought to be a corruption of an ancient field name Lady Moss which once identified an area of boggy ground a few hundred yards along this road between Hardwick's and South Lodge and the old windmill.

The Round House, Hadnall, 1917. Situated on Mill Lane, just off the A49 to the north of the village, the windmill was built in 1787 and remodelled for domestic purposes around the outbreak of the Second World War. Of red brick, with tapering sides, the building has a Gothic look about it with its round-arched window casements. Rumour has it that it was built by Viscount Rowland Hill as a commemoration of this General's exploits at Waterloo. However, it is much more likely to have been altered on his instructions soon after that famous and historically important battle of 1815. It is unlikely to have ever been a working windmill.

Shrewsbury Road, Shawbury, 1911. Mrs Jane Clowes' corner shop stands in the far distance and the local coalman delivers fuel by horse and cart whilst his customers do their best to block his access by having a good natter. 'Banky' Foulkes lived in one of the cottages on the right and from the day that the Midland Red Bus Company decided to place a bus stop near his front entrance gate, he was continually having trouble. He objected to the way that courting couples, whilst waiting to catch a bus back into Shrewsbury, could not resist a little bit of night-time canoodling in his privet hedge. Fed up with this, he eventually took matters into his own hands and painted his boundary hedge with tar.

Shawbury Women's Club. A high tea get-together on the lawn at the Elephant and Castle in 1954. This photograph, taken by Mrs Gladys Lewis, shows a few of the local lasses about to sit down at one of their summer meetings. The ladies include Mrs Venables (later of the post office), Mrs Lily Rothwell, Mrs Jessie Dickerson, Mrs Nel Brown, Mrs Dodd, Mrs Vaughan (schoolmaster's wife), Mrs Tudor and Mrs Porter.

The Elephant and Castle, Shawbury, 1956. The proprietor Charlie Lewis and his wife Gladys pose for the camera with their granddaughter, Gillian, on a garden seat at the rear of the premises.

Stanton Mill, 1905. This view, taken from the mill bridge, shows the miller's house of around 1835 with its water wheel still in full operation. The Jeffrey's family were the grain millers here for the first thirty years of the twentieth century. From the Second World War the mill was operated by Leslie Danells and his family. Complete closure came in 1954. Daughter Leslie remembers the periodic dressing of the millstones and the metal eel trap placed directly under the millwheel.

Stanton upon Hine Heath, 1930. George Rhodes had moved his bakery and general provisions business to newly-built premises here in around 1925. The Model A Ford delivery van, registration UX 9045, waits for its next trip down country lanes to the many rural customers. The staff posing for their photograph are Eddie Machin, Cyril Wynn, George Rhodes I – all bakers – Mary Mountford, Sally Rhodes (George's daughter) and Queenie Rhodes (Sally's daughter). Alf, George's son, was later to take over the running of the business. When it closed around 1990, the shop was used as a sub-post office for a few years.

Stanton upon Hine Heath, 1957. Jim Rhodes takes time off from deliveries to pose alongside his Fordson van with members of a local family – the Pointers. The van, registration FAW 721, was formerly operated by the Belle Vue Laundry before adaptation for use as a mobile shop.

Harcourt Manor, Stanton, 1906. Just prior to the taking of this photograph, George and Alice Meredith, the parents of Mary Webb, Shropshire's own novelist, were resident here, being the occupiers from 1896-1902. This red brick, late Georgian house was then known as the Woodlands, which the Meredith's acknowledged as 'being five miles from anywhere but very close to the magical follies of Hawkstone'. Whilst here Mary as a teenager wrote articles for the Stanton Parish Magazine.

Right: Ellerdine, 13 June 1916. George Rhodes stands outside the Royal Oak Inn – known locally as the Tiddlywink presumably because of its small size. George started his bakery business here in around 1895 in adjacent premises. The family was later to own bakeries in at least six different villages in Shropshire and the Marches.

Below: George Rhodes' delivery cart, Ellerdine, 1920. George's son, Alf, is about to step down from the delivery cart to make a delivery to another of his customers. The writing on the side of the cart reads 'Ellerdine Hot Air Bakery, G. Rhodes, Baker and Confectioner'.

Roden Mill, *c.* 1930. This late eighteenth-century watermill of whitewashed brick with its gabled wheel housing to the south west was operated in the 1930s by Ebeneezer Evans on behalf of the Manchester Co-operative Wholesale Society as part of their estate holding at nearby Roden. The mill house is contemporary with the mill; the whole complex survives. Always described by the Co-op as Roden, it is perhaps more generally referred to as High Ercall, being equidistant between the two.

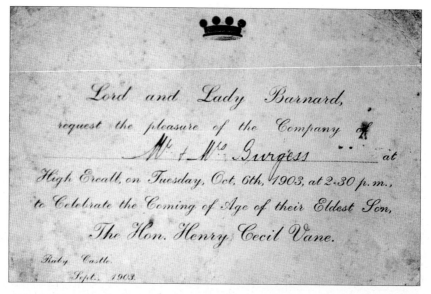

Twenty-first birthday invitation, 1903. The Vane family had lived at Raby Castle, County Durham since 1624, assuming the titles of Lords Barnard in 1698 and Dukes of Cleveland in the nineteenth century. During Victoria's reign the family owned vast tracts of land over much of mid- and north Shropshire. Mr David Burgess, to whom the invitation was sent, was employed by Lord Barnard on his High Ercall Estate as a Waggoner, although he was very much a skilled man, a general factotum, able to carry out any task asked of him, from dairyman to ploughman and from shepherd to hedge pleacher and fence erector.

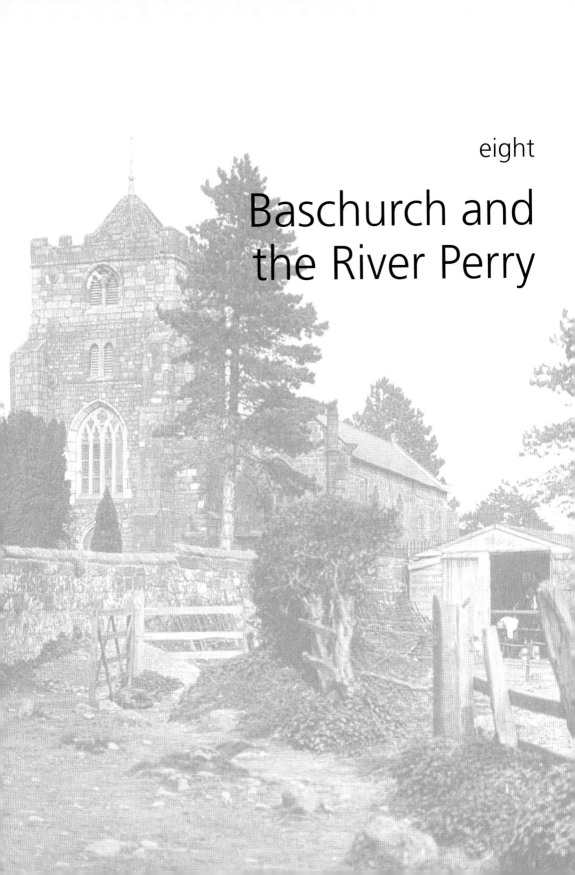

eight

Baschurch and the River Perry

Derivation of local place names:

Mytton: A river-junction settlement, referring to the confluence of the Rivers Perry and Severn.

Baschurch: Bascherche at Domesday when the church of Bassa was one of very few churches in Shropshire. Derivation from Old English, the personal name *Bas(s)a* and *cirice* for church.

The small medieval community of Baschurch, and its satellites Newtown and Prescott, was centred around the ancient church of All Saints. Much was to change. The railway arrived in 1848, the motorcar half-a-century later and the quiet, cosy country idyll eventually expanded into a vibrant large commuter village.

Food for MAN AND BEAST
TIMMIS & TUDOR

Mytton Flour Mills, Montford Bridge; Hadnall Mills, Hadnall, SALOP

Phone Nos.:
MONTFORD BRIDGE 244

HADNALL 204

●

HELP YOURSELF.

We Buy and We Sell

QUALITY—We make only the Best (A little bit of what you fancy does you good). SERVICE—Personal. DELIVERY—Prompt, by our own transport
Visit our Mills to see your Grain made into THE BEST FLOUR
CAL-O-LAC — We stock this famous Milk Saver

Timmis & Tudor, Mytton Mill, 1925. In the early years saddle-stones were used by the farmer's wife to grind the wheat, followed later by horses and what was referred to as a ginney-ring. It was not long before water was harnessed to produce the necessary power and many small enterprises began to spring up along quite minor watercourses. The waterwheel drove the large circular millstones, thus making the process of grinding that much faster. In Shropshire, many smaller mills, like the one at Redhill (Hookagate) continued until the outbreak of Second World War, but only four were operating on a commercial scale. Mytton Mill continued until around 1965 and the premises are now a thriving business park.

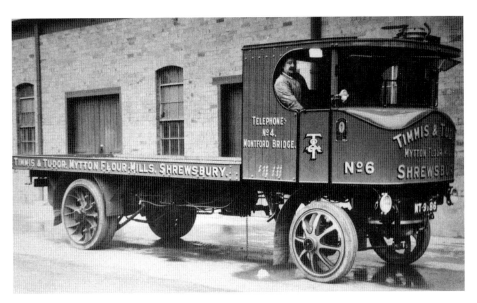

Mytton Mill, 1926. Locally engineered at Alley and Maclellan's Works on Whitchurch Road, this Super Sentinel steam wagon, registration NT 9186, was purchased by Timmis & Tudor in October 1926. Note the solid rubber tyres. Mytton Mill was on the River Perry, between Baschurch and Montford Bridge. Here, as elsewhere, electric power was utilised from the 1930s as a quicker and less troublesome alternative means of driving the numerous cogs, gears and pulleys to produce flour, balanced animal feeds, barley meal and bran.

Timmis & Tudor flour millers, Mytton. In the 1950s this 'A' Series ERF lorry, fleet no.12, was used by Timmis & Tudor to move cereals from farm to mill and from mills to the docks at Liverpool for export. The lorry is in a restored condition. One notable driver who was working from Mytton Mill at this time was Jack Robb, an employee of long service who in all probability drove this particular vehicle.

Above: Prescott House, Baschurch. The house has changed very little since this postcard was produced, just prior to the First World War, surprisingly even the finial-topped porch remains extant. The property has been the home of the Bradley family for many decades and they continue to run their building business from the adjoining workshops. These premises are known to have previously been occupied by a long line of craftsmen, dating back to the construction of two and four-wheeled carriages. The known artisans include James Payne and his son Eldred, one of which is believed to be pictured here with his wife in the front garden; George and Ellen Deborah Miles were to follow from the late 1920s.

Right: Baschurch, Prescott, *c.* 1932. This photograph is believed to show the workshop adjoining Prescott House at the time that it was operated by George Miles. Tradesmen known to have been employed there at this time include Harold Johnson (wheelwright), Jack Worrall (blacksmith) Stephen Pugh (joiner) and James Dorricott (joiner). The latter is shown to the left, axe in hand; he was killed whilst on active service in Second World War and his name appears on the parish war memorial.

Baschurch smithy, 1912. There were at least three blacksmith's shops in the Baschurch and Newtown area during the first decades of the twentieth century. This photograph shows the smithy on the Newtown road where the petrol service station now stands. The name of the lady standing in the doorway is not known but Wallace Phillips was resident blacksmith here at this time, to be followed later by members of the Passant family.

All Saints and Moor Farm, Baschurch. This photograph, taken in April 1938, shows the blacksmith's shop (on the right) at Cecil Timmis' Moor Farm, a property which is to be sold for redevelopment for housing use (2004). The yew tree (on the left) survives and the public footpath still crosses All Saints churchyard and down the dilapidated stone steps, through the boundary wall and out across the fields to Milford.

Newtown Road, Baschurch, 1935. Surprisingly little has changed since this photograph was taken near to the White House – the premises behind the large gates on the left, which was then the residence of Ted Lewis, a local butcher. The shop sign of the Onions Bros – Bill and Charlie, butchers and grocers, can be seen beyond the Morris Eight car; whilst in Church Road to the left was yet another butchers shop. The roof of the Methodist church (built 1873) can be seen in the background on the right. Eyton Lane turns to the right and the long-established primary school which dates back to 1709 and the Eleanor Harris Charity. Significant extensions took place here in 1870. Further down the road in more recent times the Corbett Secondary School was established.

The Admiral Duncan, Baschurch, c. 1905. It has not been possible to put an exact date to this postcard but it would seem that some kind of re-enactment of coaching days was taking place here. Four replacement horses have been or are about to be harnessed, the inn at this time having stabling facilities for ten horses. The Duncan was established from around 1800 and the present frontage shows little change apart from a new entrance porch and alterations to the windows including a new one in the arched recess to the left.

Baschurch, Elmhurst, *c.* 1920. It is understood that this family photograph shows Andrew Hamilton, the local veterinary surgeon, outside Elmhurst, his Station Road residence, with his wife Elizabeth Jane and child. The car is a Model T Ford, all spruced up with its brass radiator cover and acetylene lamps, and the variant is likely to be a 1915 Coupelet. Andrew Hamilton was in partnership with John Higginson but in around 1926 Mr Higginson moved to Knockin and set up in practice on his own account.

Village shop, Station Road, Baschurch, 1908. As with other villages of its size, Baschurch once had several small retail businesses serving its population. One such shop was that run by Fox-Davies and Passmore until 1912 and is shown here with various employees posing for the cameraman. Much altered, it was later under the direction of John Edward Francis; in more recent times Campbell Keay and also Malcolm Fisher. It now serves as the sub-post office. A postcard of the premises sent to Mr B. Feltus of no. 14 School Lane, Belle Vue, Shrewsbury, has a rather pleading message reading 'Mr Griffiths asks me to ask you if you will play cricket for Weston against Belvidere on the Gay Meadow on Thursday next?'

Left: Slater's Farm, Baschurch, 1920. Full of smiles and apparently ready for work as a dairymaid at New Buildings Farm on the Ruyton XI Towns road, this snapshot shows 'Ginty' Gwilt carrying her stool and bucket. Hand milking was common practice up until the outbreak of Second World War and at many smaller farms for some years afterwards.

Below: Baschurch rail crash. A serious railway accident occurred at Baschurch Station on the evening of 13 February 1961. A northbound freight train was reversing into a refuge siding at the south end of the station when a following express passenger train, having been given clearance to proceed, ploughed into the front of the freight which, due to human error, had mistakenly started to pull out onto the main line. Three men were killed including the driver and fireman of the passenger train and a railway stores attendant in the van immediately behind the locomotive.

Marton Hall, 1935. Situated almost equidistance between Baschurch and Myddle, Marton Hall appears at first sight to be an imposing example of Elizabethan architecture. It is not exactly a disappointment, however, to discover that the building dates from 1914, for the architectural detail and workmanship is first class. The tiled roof and the mullioned and transomed windows are impressive but the local friable red sandstone (Shelvock Quarry) blocks are already showing signs of serious weather spalling. Now the home of the Gwilt family.

Dame Agnes Hunt and Emily Selina Goodford. Dame Agnes was born in 1867 at Boreatton Park, the daughter of Rowland Hunt and his wife Marianne. After training at hospitals in Rhyl, Hammersmith and Shrewsbury RSI; she formed a close working relationship in the 1890s with a fellow nurse, Emily Selina Goodford. After further work in Northamptonshire, Middlesbrough and Nottinghamshire, Agnes returned to Shropshire with Emily. In 1903, Agnes, due to problems of her own with an infected hip joint, was to meet the Liverpool Consulting Surgeon, Robert Jones. Emily Goodford died in 1920 and Dame Agnes Hunt in 1948.

Florence House, Baschurch, 1912. This large private house was purchased by the Hunt family in 1900 with a view to adapting it for use as a convalescent home, to be managed by Agnes Hunt and Emily Woodford. The home was opened on 1 October, with 'open sheds' for their patients. The chance meeting, three years later with Robert Jones led directly to the establishment of an orthopaedic hospital at Florence House, with patients being operated on by surgeons at the Royal South Liverpool Hospital. Later these functions were carried out in Baschurch, the kitchen table being brought into use.

Baschurch convalescent home. This photograph from 1914 shows the open-air treatment wards and a selection of what appears to be soldiers convalescing after treatment for their war injuries. Tents were also erected on the lawns for this purpose. From 1917 children suffering from surgical tuberculosis were accepted for treatment and funds began to accumulate, eventually enabling the purchase of the former military hospital Park Hall.

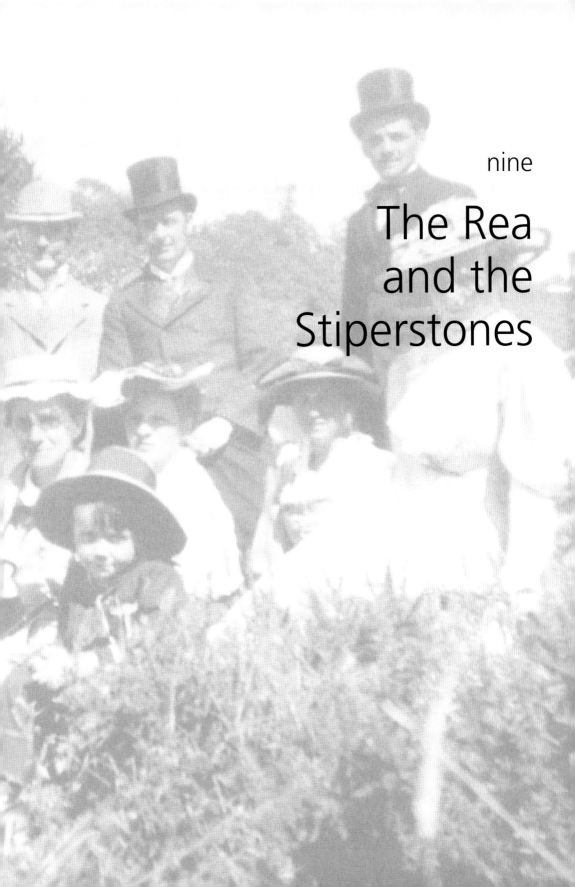

nine

The Rea and the Stiperstones

Derivation of local place names:

Hanwood: *Hanewde* at Domesday. The 'wood' element rather speaks for itself but the *Hana* factor is more problematical; could mean a domestic cock, a rock or an Old English personal name.

Plealey: Previously 'Pleleye' and 'Plalegh', and Plealey from 1615. Derivation from 'plega' and 'leah' – a clearing for sport.

Pontesbury: From 'pont' a bridge or more likely from *Pant*, an Old English personal name.

Minsterley: Formerly part of the ancient parish and minster church of Westbury, within an afforested area.

Snailbeach: Believed to originate from batch meaning a deep valley. The 'snail' element is anyone's guess, perhaps a plague of molluscs!

Hope Valley: More correctly, the Valley of Hope, from a Celtic derivation.

Hanwood village shop. The proprietor, Frederick William Mansell, and his father, Ernest Walter, stand chatting to an unknown visitor in front of his premises in 1936. It would seem that Mr Mansell sold everything from Oxo cubes to bicycles.

Above: Hanwood Rovers FC, *c.* 1900. Once
a coalmining village, Hanwood could always
boast a high calibre amateur football team.
Their prowess was so renowned locally that
they were always known as the team to beat.
The players and officials of this particular team
are, from left to right: Mr Sam Coles;
J. Wheatley; J. Tomlins; J. Tipton; –?–; E. Cooper,
H. Edwards (Treasurer). Middle Row:
W. Edwards; W. Tipton; W. Davies. Front row:
C. Powis; P. Randles; C. Crowther; A. Harrison;
–?–.

Right: PC Thomas Richard Perry, *c.* 1925.
PC Perry was educated at Cruckmeole School
and in 1901, at the age of twenty-five, joined
the Metropolitan Police. He retired in 1926,
having been presented with long service and
Coronation medals. He returned to his roots
where he lived at no. 7 Arscott, Pontesford,
with Mrs Elsie Clowes, a local shopkeeper. He
died on 17 July 1941, age sixty-five, and was
buried at Pontesbury.

Spencer Lodge, Plealey, *c.* 1930. Major Herbert John Hill is pictured with his trusty spaniel outside his late eighteenth century brick-built property in the period between the wars. The slim Tuscan-pilastered entrance is shown with its semi-circular fanlight.

The Nag's Head, Pontesford, 1905. William Davies, who had just taken over the tenancy from his father, Samuel, was a licensed brewer as well as a retailer of beer and spirits. The building, owned by Mr Heighway Jones of nearby Earlsdale, had stabling for seven horses. It dates from the early nineteenth century and the round-headed windows with lozenge glazing within rectangular reveals, today remain a distinctive feature. The ramshackle canopy has long since disappeared.

The Nills, Pontesbury, *c.* 1935. Situated on Pontesbury Hill at the north-east end of the Stiperstones range, Nills Cottage was the second local home of Mary Webb and her husband, Henry Meredith. It was here that she wrote *Gone to Earth.* The Meredith's first came to Pontesbury in 1914 taking up the tenancy of Rose Cottage, Hinton Road, but within two years had found the annual rent of £36 too much of a burden. They moved to the Nills in 1916. Early in 1917 family finances had improved and a new property, Spring Cottage on Lyth Hill, soon beckoned.

Dr Wilfred Jameson the local GP for the Pontesbury area, together with his family as they appeared on a Christmas card of 1905. Dr Jameson, from County Carlow, Ireland, and his wife Edith, came to Pontesbury in 1898 and set up in practice at Cliffdale. They had four children, losing the first two, twins, in infancy. Molly, the next child, was to train as a nurse and died on 10 May 1928 at Buenos Aires whilst serving on RMS *Franconia*. She was thirty-one. The youngest daughter, Mona, always known as Mosie, was to run a school at Cliffdale into the 1930s. A niece, Miss Doris Tuthill, also pictured, spent long periods at the Jameson's and was later to help Mona at the school. The children's nanny is the other lady standing in the picture. Dr Jameson died in 1929, age sixty-five, and his wife, Edith, in 1943 at the age of eighty-two.

Above: Bennett's stores, Pontesbury. The postcard is dated 1908 when Edwin Bennett managed proceedings in the shop, ably assisted by his daughter, Clara. There was also a Wilfred Bennett who was in charge of warehousing and deliveries. The bakery was a thriving concern with orders for bread and confectionery being dealt with by horse and cart, covering a wide area. The identities of the bakers pictured are not known but some who served their apprenticeship amongst the coke-fired ovens were Bert Challinor, Ron Challinor, brothers Alan and Les Rowson, Clarence Kinsey, Ken Jones, Charlie Jones, Jack Johnson, Arthur Lunn and Jimmy Stephens. The premises now form part of the Spar chain of stores.

Left: Hugleth Barytes Mine, 1912. The miner on the right is Samuel Rogers. He was not to realise it but in very quick time he was to find himself in the 6 Battalion of the KSLI as no. 11580 Private Rogers. He was later to be killed on the Somme battlefield on 3 August 1916, aged twenty-one, and is buried at the Sucrerie Military Cemetery at Colincamp, west of Bapaume, Flanders. The name of the other miner is not known. Hugleth Mine had opened in 1910 and soon proved to be very productive. Situated on the east side of the Stiperstones ridge and beyond Habberley village, it was provided with an overhead ropeway in 1918 which ran for some three-and-a-half miles to barytes processing mill at Malehurst near Pontesbury.

Lewis Bros, Minsterley, transport contractors. This local haulier purchased numerous steam wagons and trailers for their transport business. This Sentinel DG4 platform-back waggons of around 1930, Lewis Fleet no. 7, has pneumatic tyres and is photographed outside Sentinel's factory in Whitchurch Road, Shrewsbury.

Minsterley Creameries Ltd, c. 1958. A Morris Commercial delivery lorry being stacked high with a load of Shropshire cheeses. The creamery was founded in 1902 and was first situated to the south west of the village on the road to Hope Valley. Expansion necessitated a move to the present site adjacent to the former railway station. Changes in ownership, constant product updating and much diversification eventually led to the concentration of output on yoghurt and similar products.

Lordshill Baptist Chapel, Snailbeach. This postcard dated 29 December 1904 is intriguing in many ways, none more so than because of the message written by the sender. It reads 'Passive Register. Thought this picture would interest you as it is a view of the local minister outside the chapel refusing to pay the Education Rate'. It is presumed that payment is being refused to the Government's tax collector! The minister's daughter watches the cameraman as does the collector. A publicity stunt by the minister perhaps! This chapel was the scene of the public baptism of Hazel Woodhouse (Jennifer Jones) by her husband, Edward Marston (Cyril Cusack) in the film adaptation of Mary Webb's novel *Gone to Earth*.

Gone to Earth, amateur film extras, 1949. This snapshot shows a gathering of some of the local talent dressed up in all their finery of the 1890s. The film was *Gone to Earth*. It must have been great fun dressing up each day at Minsterley Village Hall. Transportation followed by bus to the film set wherever that might be. Those lucky enough to be part of the proceedings included: Walton Humphrey, Beatty, Sylvia, Terence and Ken to name but a few of the Jones', Doreen, Dorothy, Alice and Chrissie Rowson, Mavis France, Lydia and Thelma Harrison, plus a good sprinkling of Purslow's, Evans', Lewis', Edwards' and Hayward's. There was even another Betty Davies!

Right: Snailbeach, 1906. Miss Rose Helena Rawlings poses for her father, Joseph Rawlings of Cressage, in front of George's Pit headstock with the narrow gauge railway lines running alongside. The spoil heaps containing galena ore and barytes are much in evidence.

Below: Snailbeach Post Office and shop, 1913. Situated in a central position alongside the main road to the Stiperstones, it must have been a focal point for the exchange of pleasantries and local tittle-tattle when the sub-post mistress, Hannah Rowson, was in charge of transactions.

Roundhill Mine, 1908. Situated approximately one third of mile from the Tankerville complex and south west of Stiperstones village, Roundhill was always a stop start venture. The mine had reopened in 1906 for the umpteenth time, only to close yet again in 1913. Further extraction of barytes took place in the 1920s. This looks rather a busy scene, the steam pumping engine within its new corrugated iron-clad shed, appears to be an excellent attempt at clearing the underground workings of water. Miners stand on the head frame watching proceedings.

The Stiperstones Inn. Looking north and down the valley with Oak Hill in the background. White-washed walls and a new entrance porch have since changed the appearance of the hostelry. The writer of the postcard in August 1937 had just sampled the inn's hospitality, no doubt generated by Mrs Esther Humphreys who at that time was the licensee.

Above: The Sun Inn, The Gravels, Hope Valley, 1912. George Jones, licensee, was responsible for filling the ale jugs as local smallholders dropped by in their horse-drawn transport. In this quiet, rural setting, shanks' pony would have been the normal means of getting about. The photographer, Alfred Wright of Shrewsbury, had lined up the imbibers, many being lead and barytes miners, for this snapshot. All no doubt would have first insisted on quenching their thirst! The Sun is believed to have closed its doors for the last time in around 1935, when virtually all mineral extraction hereabouts had finished. The inn, which more than likely was originally a farmhouse, then reverted back to domestic use.

Right: Edmund Ashworth, clog man. A well-known character of the 1920s and '30s who lived at Drury Lane, Plox Green, Mr Ashworth served with the Royal Flying Corps during First World War. Leaving his wife to tend to the smallholding, he was to spend his working day on the banks of the Rea or Cound. Wearing his distinctive breeches, gaiters and flat cap, he was kept busy felling alders, sawing and shaping them into oblong blocks, either eight inches, nine inches or ten inches in length by six inches wide and two inches thick. Each clog size was achieved by the use of the long, wide blade illustrated in the photograph. Loosely attached by a hook to a small workbench, Mr Ashworth always referred to this implement as his 'monkey's tail'. The alder tree felling always opened up new vistas, more especially at Hookagate and Dorrington. After drying out in large piles at the brook side, the blocks were taken away by Dick Robinson, haulage contractor of Minsterley, to Central Lancashire for finishing.

Other local titles published by Tempus

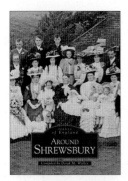

Around Shrewsbury
DEREK M. WALLEY

This book examines the different aspects of life in a mainly agricultural community and shows the numerous changes in local streets, schools, churches and factories that were produced by social and economic progress, which was often both spectacular and memorable. This collection of old photographs and postcards will bring back memories of history of Shrewsbury and is a good companion volume to *Around Shrewsbury Volume II*.
07524 1675 8

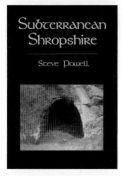

Subterranean Shropshire
STEVE POWELL

Shropshire has its fair share of 'secret subterranean tunnels', most of these having a basis in the imagination of the storyteller, but some, including such features as the ice houses, cave cottages, rock houses, tunnels, mine ventures, underground temples, grottoes and ornamental caves described in this book, played a major part in variously providing an underground world of housing, food storage, religious sanctity or entertaining eccentricity in times past.
07524 2761 X

Folklore of the Welsh Border
JACQUELINE SIMPSON

The Welsh Border is a region rich in folklore. This study explores traditional folk tales and beliefs, including stories of giants and ghosts, witches and fairies. These stories, arising from ancient beliefs and originating in an oral tradition of storytelling, are tales relating to local monuments and tales explaining some of the local traditions that are still upheld in the twenty-first century.
07524 2623 0

Soldiers of Shropshire
PETER DUCKERS FOR THE SHROPSHIRE REGIMENTAL MUSEUM

For generations, the county of Shropshire had maintained a range of military units – infantry, cavalry, artillery, medical and the rest – which have served effectively and loyally in peacetime and in war. This book presents a selection of photographs of these 'part-time' soldiers of Shropshire between 1870 and 1970. It offers a glimpse of the county's local volunteer regiments on ceremonial duty, on active service and in training.
07524 1866 1

If you are interested in purchasing other books published by Tempus, or in case you have difficulty finding any Tempus books in your local bookshop, you can also place orders directly through our website
www.tempus-publishing.com